Recovery the Native Way

A Therapist's Manual

Recovery the Native Way

A Therapist's Manual

by

Alf H. Walle
Ilisagvik College Barrow, Alaska

Information Age Publishing, Inc.
Charlotte, North Carolina • www.infoagepub.com

ISBN 13: 978-1-59311-833-4

Printed in the United States of America

Dedication

This book is dedicated to those who seek to develop strategies of therapy that are aimed toward the special needs of Native people who seek to use their cultures, heritage, and traditions as tools of recovery.

CONTENTS

CONTENTS

Foreword

In recent years, there has been a growing awareness that Native clients who suffer from substance abuse often face challenges that are distinct from those experienced by the mainstream population.

For past decade, I have been involved in research involving Native alcoholism and I have recently published a book on the subject titled *The Path of Handsome Lake: A Model of Recovery for Native People.* My book argues that many different Native cultures (in America and elsewhere) face similar challenges and disruptions because their cultures are often under great stress and/or because people are alienated from their heritage. The dysfunctional responses of many different Native peoples are similar because they are subjected to similar pressures.

In a nutshell, due to contact with the outside world, Native cultures often experience disruptive pressures, and (in some instances) entire cultures or ways of life may face extinction. Under such circumstances, the culture loses the ability to help people cope with the pressures of life. Cultural decline itself often causes additional trauma. Combined, these pressures trigger dysfunction within the Native community.

The obvious antidote for such maladies is to help Native substance abusers to reconnect with their heritage in positive and constructive ways. My earlier book and this one are inspired by the life and work of nineteenth century Iroquois leader Handsome Lake who developed a method to help Native people embrace their heritage as they recovered from substance abuse.

Because my earlier book was scholarly and not focused on practitioner issues, using it within a therapeutic context may be difficult. Here, I adapt my ideas so they can be applied to therapy in a systematic and productive manner. The total program of therapy is presented in three volumes. The first is a short overview of the program that has been written at about a 10th-grade reading level. My goal is to provide a wide range of clients (as well as those who pursue self-help work) with an easily understood description of the program. The second volume is a consumable workbook designed to be used alongside the reader. The workbook can serve both within the context of therapy and by those seeking strategies of self-help.

The volume you are reading is a guide for therapists to consult when using this method to help Native clients. It is hoped that all three of these texts will play a significant role in the therapy and recovery of Native substance abusers.

Preface

Native substance abuse is a profound problem. It is also a malady that is often poorly addressed by "generic" therapies that have been developed within the mainstream world. My earlier book, *The Path of Handsome Lake: A Model of Recovery for Native People*, as well as this book (and the other two volumes in this series), are designed to deal with these issues in a culturally appreciative manner that helps Native people recover from substance abuse. The two other books in this series include a description of the program written at a 10th-grade level for clients to read and a consumable workbook for people seeking recovery to use along with the aforementioned reader.[1]

Many therapies seek to help people recover from substance abuse or alcoholism and to lead productive and fulfilling lives. The better known of these therapies (such as the Twelve Steps program), however, stem from the experiences of mainstream people. While such tools are useful, they do not actively address the fact that the traditional cultures of Native People are often weakened and/or specific individuals may be alienated from their heritage. Many Native people suffer because their world has changed and/or that they feel they have little place in it. These hurtful feelings and the resulting sense of alienation can trigger dysfunction. Mainstream programs of recovery, unfortunately, covertly assume that, once people recover, their culture will be available to re-embrace them and provide the comfort and support they need.

Such assumptions are contradicted by the experiences of many Native people. Indeed, massive cultural change and/or a weakening of traditions are often the initial catalyst that leads to substance abuse in the first place. Or, perhaps, people have become alienated from their traditions in hurtful ways that led to dysfunction. In such cases (so commonplace within the Native community), the traditional culture and/or the individual's relationship to it may be severely weakened. Perhaps a traditional heritage may not be available to provide strength and coping skills. The relationship with the traditional heritage is often a weak link in a Native substance abuser's life that needs to be addressed. Due to this reality, I wrote my scholarly book *The Path of Handsome Lake: A Model of Recovery for Native People* (2004), as well as the three volumes in this series.

This book begins with background information including an overview of theories and methods regarding Native substance. This discussion demonstrates that many therapy programs developed for Native people revolve around reconnecting people with their roots in a positive and constructive way. This book is a part of this emerging tradition of therapy.

In chapter 2, "The Handsome Lake Method: An Introduction" the particular method employed is discussed. (The reader is encouraged to read the full description of the method in my scholarly book *The Path of Handsome Lake: A Model of Recovery for Native People*.) The overview included here provides the bare skeleton that is needed to follow my chain of thought. In essence, the program encourages people to reconnect with their heritage in positive and therapeutic ways.

Having presented an overview of the method, the book provides an array of suggestions for treatment that are based on this culturally sensitive framework. Chapter 3 provides a formal discussion of strategies, while chapter 4 provides more ad hoc suggestions. Although individual therapists will, no doubt, evolve their own strategies of treatment, I hope that by providing a few initial suggestions, they can quickly adjust to the program.

One of the realities of substance abuse therapy is that assessment precedes treatment. The diagnosis, furthermore, impacts the treatment options that are made available to the individual. The program of therapy that is encouraged here is based on the fact that many Native people suffer due to a weakening of their culture and/or an alienation from it. Unfortunately, the *Diagnostic and Statistical Manual of Mental Disorders* (DSM-IV), that provides the commonly used framework for the diagnosis and evaluation of clients, is not specifically geared toward this type of issue. As a result, therapists often lack the tools they need to adequately document the culturally driven issues that Native clients face.

In chapter 5, "Adjusting the DSM Diagnostic Criteria to Deal With Native Clients," this problem is addressed. I hope that my discussion will help therapists use the DSM-IV in order to justify therapy that is hinged around cultural issues involving Native clients.

After discussing a way to upgrade the DSM-IV to better serve Native clients, chapter 6 provides a more "hands on" application of how a more culturally sensitive DSM-IV can be used in the actual diagnosis and evaluation of clients. It is hoped that this chapter will effectively translate theory to practice.

Having presented a way to better adjust the DSM-IV to deal with Native cultural issues, chapter 7 provides sample treatment plans that employ the Handsome Lake method. In specific, two 12-week treatment plans (one for individuals, the other for group therapy) are provided. Although, no doubt, each therapist will want to craft their own unique applications of the method, it is hoped that these examples will be illustrative and useful.

To a large extent, this book is the product of the experiences of Native Americans and Native Alaskans. As a result, the reader might initially assume that my findings would be culture bound and applicable only to Native people from this part of the world. In reality, the method has been designed to be an appropriate therapy for a wide range of Native peoples. While specific Native cultures throughout the world are unique and distinct, the pressures they face due to contact with the outside world are often very similar. In innumerable cases, outside intervention triggers massive changes and losses. And these alterations in the traditional way of life (and/or the individual's relationship to it) are often the catalyst for dysfunctional behavior, such as substance abuse.

In order to make this program as broad based as possible, I have worked examples of other cultural traditions (such as Native Hawaiians and the Maori of New Zealand) into my discussion. Those comparisons are much more prominent in my scholarly book than here, but references to these parallels remain. Many Native cultures face threats and pressures from the outside world. As a result, many Native cultures have trouble serving the needs of some (or all) of their members. When such situations exist, people become vulnerable to dysfunction. Antidotes for this dysfunction include strengthening the Native culture and/or rebuilding the individual's relationship to it.

This book is designed to provide therapists with the tools they need to help clients use their traditional heritage as tools of recovery. It is hoped that these tools will facilitate employing a culturally appropriate therapy aimed at Native clients.

NOTE

1. These valuable tools are available through Information Age Publishing, the publisher of this volume. In chapter 8, treatment plans based on those books are presented in detail.

Prologue to Part 1

Increasingly substance abuse therapists recognize that Native people may experience both alcoholism and recovery in ways that are different from other people. Chapter 1 provides an overview of various theories that exist regarding Native alcoholism. Both biological and social/cultural explanations have been raised and both theories have a significant following among professionals. These two causes, furthermore, are not inherently mutually exclusive; thus, they can impact people simultaneously. While biological factors may be present, this book focuses primarily on social impacts that can trigger substance abuse. It is my belief that Native cultures are often under attack by outside social and economic forces and/or many Native people have become alienated from their heritage. This situation can cause stress that triggers substance abuse.

Besides dealing with substance abuse among Native people, chapter 1 documents how many Native treatment programs seek to help Native people recover by embracing their culture, traditions, and heritage.

Chapter 1

Substance Abuse and Native People

Substance abuse is complicated. When dealing with specific groups, such as Native populations, the issues multiply. This book emphasizes that substance abuse and recovery among Native people is apt to be distinct from what is observed in the mainstream population. This perspective rebuts from those who suggest that substance abuse is a universal malady that impacts all people in similar ways (and can best be treated using generic, "one size fits all" programs of recovery.)

Substance abuse among Native Americans is recognized as a major problem even though theories regarding this phenomenon vary. While the stereotype of the "drunken Indian" is most distasteful, few challenge the observation that many Native Americans are substance abusers. A number of theories attempt to explain why this is true. Current thinking points to both biological and cultural explanations. Here, both perspectives are discussed.

BIOLOGICAL ARGUMENTS

A prevailing theory (often dubbed the "firewater myth") suggests that Native people tend to be vulnerable to alcoholism for genetic reasons. This theory is supported by much anecdotal evidence. In any event, many Native people exhibit heavy and uncontrolled drinking (Mail & Johnson 1993.)

The firewater myth goes back hundreds of years. Both Benjamin Franklin and members of the Lewis and Clark expedition observed that Native Americans habitually drank to excess and that violence frequently erupted as a result (Duran & Duran, 1995).

Over the years, there has been much discussion regarding the vulnerability of Native Americans to alcoholism. One classic evolutionary argument begins by recalling that in many parts of the world (such as Europe and the Middle East), alcoholic beverages have been available for thousands of years. As a result, the logic continues, over many generations, alcoholics and people with alcoholic parents were at a competitive disadvantage and, therefore, they had a lower chance of surviving and reproducing. Based on this observation, some researchers conclude that in places where alcoholic beverages have long been present evolutionary forces reduced the frequency of genes that created a biologically vulnerability to alcohol.

In the Americas, in contrast, there was no widespread use of alcoholic beverages until the era of White contact. (The only example of Native Americans consuming alcoholic beverages of which the author is aware is the custom of fermenting the sap of the Sugar Maple tree during the spring in the northeastern portion of North America.) Those practicing this tradition, however, only produced a mildly alcoholic beverage that was only available during a short period of the year (a situation that would prevent the onslaught of full-blown alcoholism).

Because alcohol was not available to precontact Native Americans, the forces of evolution would not have reduced the tendency toward alcoholism. Once alcoholic beverages became available to the Native population, therefore, the impact was devastating.

Biological theories regarding other ailments exist. Although the common cold is merely a minor annoyance for most White people, it initially ravaged American Indians as a deadly plague because the Native population had not evolved any resistance to a disease that previously did not exist in America. The same reasoning can be used to explain a Native vulnerability to alcoholic beverages.

Nonetheless, adequately and rigorously researching such theories using the scientific method is difficult, if not impossible (Snipp, 1997). And as Garcia-Andrade, Wall, and Ehlers have observed (1997), there is no evidence that demonstrates that Native Americans have a higher psychological or physiological tendency toward alcoholism than any other group of people. Bolstering such observations, Mail and Johnson (1993) note that drinking patterns vary widely among various Native American groups and no stereotyped pattern can be discerned.

THE IMPACT OF CULTURE AND SOCIETY

Other theories link alcoholic tendencies among Native Americans to cultural and social factors. Some researchers observe that Native Americans have a strong tradition of employing mind-altering substances within a ceremonial setting (Abbott, 1996) while others suggest that Native Americans often seek transcendental encounters and that mind-altering-substances are often used to facilitate this type of experience (Kahn, 1986; Mail & McDonald, 1980). Although these writers make some interesting points, the author intuitively senses that there is a difference between a person participating in a highly structured sacred ceremony, on the one hand, and passing out drunk in the gutter, on the other. Arguments that suggest that a precedent for alcoholism lies in the religious heritage of the various Native American peoples appear to be in conflict with one of the most respected theories on alcoholism that argues that when mind-altering substances are well integrated within a society and/or its religion, people tend to employ these drugs in relatively responsible ways. Thus, researchers often suggest that in situations where the religion of a culture provides a positive role model for a healthy use of alcohol, the incidence of abuse tends to decline.

Suggesting that the sacred use of mind-altering drugs can trigger high levels of alcohol abuse conflicts with well-established theories (mentioned above) that argue that the formal, well-organized, and ceremonial use of mind-altering substances may serve as an antidote against abuse. In specific, theories that link religious practices with substance abuse go against the grain of a significant research tradition and, therefore, they must be approached with caution.

A more plausible theory emphasizes that the impact of stigma, poverty, cultural decline, and so on, bedeviling many Native people may make them vulnerable to dysfunctional responses. Native cultures have long been subjected to profound stress and these pressures can trigger alcohol abuse. The current trends in research involving ethnic groups reinforce such perspectives. In this regard, Al-Issa (1997) emphasizes that hurtful drinking patterns among various ethnic groups may be influenced by:

1. The stress people face when living in an alien environment,
2. Socioeconomic stress including being poverty stricken, and
3. The tensions inherent in minority status.

Such perspectives form the basic underpinning of this book. Although biological arguments are not completely ruled out, this book focuses on cultural stress and its impacts upon Native people.

SPECIFIC NEEDS OF NATIVE AMERICANS

It has often been noted that many Native American substance abusers are not well served by existing strategies of recovery, such as those that are based on Alcoholics Anonymous and the Twelve Steps program. Observers routinely note that many Native people are uncomfortable with Alcoholics Anonymous and its strategy of treatment. On many occasions, Native Americans in recovery overtly complain that Alcoholics Anonymous/the Twelve Steps program does not mesh with who they are and what they experience or feel. Apparently, the Twelve Steps program does not provide a universal strategy of recovery that is suitable for all recovering individuals.

The ineffectiveness of Alcoholics Anonymous among many Native people appears to result from the fact that AA is not designed to deal with a number of problems that can trigger substance abuse among Native people. Although AA's Twelve Steps program has a valuable role to play in therapy, that method does not directly focus on the pain, cultural stress, and alienation often endured by Native people. As a result, Native clients often need to employ a different set of tools as they seek recovery.

Finding the proper program, however, can be complicated because Native Americans are, themselves, a heterogeneous group composed of many different cultures. Some Native people, furthermore live in a reservation setting while others reside within the larger community. Different individuals face a variety of pressures; a result of this diversity, no rigid program is likely to be universally applicable to all of them.

An appropriate, but flexible set of tools is needed for promoting recovery among Native Americans. This technique, however, must be able to transcend the differences between a wide range of Native American cultures, on the one hand, while dealing with the significant pressures that specific Native people face, on the other. These pressures typically include (1) the ubiquitous encroachments by the dominant culture on Native traditions, (2) economic hardships facing many Native people, and (3) the "second class citizen" status endured by many Natives.

Many Native Americans, furthermore are impacted by a process that can be described as "cultural genocide." Outsiders have often attempted to strip Native Americans of their cultural heritage. The conflict of being caught between worlds and being forced to endure the relentless undercutting of their cultural traditions has taken a great toll on many Native people. This process can inflict profound damage since a strong cultural heritage normally serves as a bulwark that binds people together and provides meaning and significance to life. Traditions that are profoundly weakened, unfortunately, cannot adequately serve this role; as a result, trauma can result. This has often been the case among Native populations.

Many therapists have recognized the fact that culture can serve as a positive force capable of providing strength, direction, and an ability to overcome dysfunction. As Beauvais has observed:

> Many Indian people believe that the loss of their culture is the primary cause of many of their existing social problems, especially those associated with alcohol. Many of the community-based alcohol treatment programs in Indian communities across the country have a strong cultural or spiritual component that is intended to revitalize traditional beliefs and serve as the primary source of individual strength in maintaining sobriety. (1998, p. 7)

Beauvais complains, however, that such phenomena are not easily measured, quantified, and examined in "scientific ways." As a result, researchers using the standard scientific approach have not been able to adequately examine such theories. This book, embracing a humanistic style of social analysis, examines these issues from a broader perspective.

It is important to recognize the degree to which traditional cultures, such as those of various Native American communities, are under attack by multiple social and economic forces. In addition, both therapists and clients need to acknowledge the important role that a viable cultural tradition can play in promoting good mental health. Unfortunately, Native American cultures are often under profound attack and the resulting stress takes an inevitable toll (if these costs can be conveniently documented using scientific/quantitative methods of analysis or not.)

These hurtful impacts should never be forgotten, even though (1) all cultures constantly evolve and (2) individuals need to respond in positive and constructive ways. While therapists urge their clients to adapt to circumstance, they should also encourage them to exercise self-determinism. One aspect of self-determinism is being able to participate in therapy that is meaningful and appropriate.

In recent years, there has been a strong movement to help members of the counseling profession to gain "multicultural counseling competencies" by (1) being aware of their own values and biases, (2) being aware of the client's world view, and (3) choosing appropriate strategies of intervention (Sue, Arredondo, & McDavis, 1992, pp. 444-446). The basic concern driving this movement is that, on many occasions, clients may not be well served by counselors and by models of intervention that are not geared to their cultural background.

Both therapists and clients, furthermore, need to recognize that cultures, although evolving, can maintain themselves and continue to function (even when specific individuals simultaneously have a niche both within the larger world and the traditional culture.) It is equally vital to remember that when individuals have a niche and a stake in two different (and potentially competing) communities, conflicts capable of triggering dysfunction can easily develop. From a more encouraging perspective, cultures can help people respond to the pressures that are faced and, therefore, offer direction and strength. By acknowledging that mental health is often profoundly (albeit subtly) intertwined with a strong and vital cultural underpinning, both therapists and clients are reminded of the connection between personal well-being and a good relationship with a viable heritage.

CONCLUDING STATEMENT

Substance abuse is a complex and multifaceted phenomenon. It is also a malady to which Native people appear to be particularly vulnerable. On the one hand, biological arguments often suggest that Native Americans are particularly vulnerable to alcoholism for genetic reasons. Cultural theories that dominate this book, in contrast, focus on a range of tensions, pressures, and stresses that can trigger dysfunction. Combined, these distinct, although interrelated, influences can be used to explain why Native people appear to be especially vulnerable to substance abuse and alcoholism.

While this book is primarily the product of my work within Native American and Native Alaskan communities, the method it presents can be applied to a wide range of Native cultures that are found throughout the world. This is because the focus of this program is on the impact of the larger world upon traditional societies, not merely on the uniqueness of any specific cultural heritage. When writing this book, I was very much aware of other cultural traditions, most specifically those of Native Hawaiians and the Moira of New Zealand. I have found that although these cultures are not closely related to those of their North American counterparts, their responses to the stress of contact and social change are largely parallel. Similar pressures, it seems, have triggered parallel responses. As a result of this fact, much of what has been developed from the American experience can be applied elsewhere.

REFERENCES

Abbot, P. J. (1996). American Indian and Alaska Native aboriginal use of alcohol in the United States. *American Indian and Alaska Native Mental Health Research, 7*(2), 1-13.

Beauvais, F. (1998). American Indians and alcohol. *Alcohol Health and Research World, 22*(4), 253-260.

Duran, E., & Duran, B. (1995). *Native American postcolonial psychology.* Albany: New York State University Press.

Garcia-Andrade, C., Wall, T. L, & Ehlers, C. L. (1997). The firewater myth and response to alcohol. *Mission Indians American Journal of Psychiarty, 154,* 983-958.

Al-Issa, I., & Oudii, S. (1997). Ethnicity, immigration, and psycholgy. In I. Al-Issa & M. Tousignant (Eds.), *Ethnicity, immigration, and psychopathology* (pp. 3-15). New York: Plenum.

Kahn, M. (1986). Psychological disorders of aboriginal people of the United States and Australia. *Journal of Rural Community Psychology, 7,* 45-59.

Mail, P. D., & Johnson, S. (1993) "Boozing, Sniffing and Toking: An Overview of Past, Present, and Future of Substance Use by American Indians. *American Indian and Alaska Mental Health Research, 5*(1), 1-33.

Mail, P. D., & McDonald, D. R. (1980). *Tulapai to Takani: A Bibliography of alcohol use and abuse among Native Americans of North America.* New Haven, CT: HRAF Press.

Sue, D. W., Arredondo, P., & McDavis, R. J. (1992). Multicultural counseling competencies and standards: A call to the profession. *Journal of Counseling and Development, 70.*

Snipp, M. (1997). Some observations about racial boundaries and the experiences of American Indians. *Ethnic and Racial Studies, 20,* 665-689.

Prologue to Part 2

After being introduced to Native alcohol therapy and the value of Native-based treatment, chapters 2 through 4 present the core of the method developed in this book. It is based on the example of Handsome Lake, a nineteenth century Iroquois leader who developed a strategy of recovery through cultural renewal. This method is strengthened by the fact that contemporary Native people (such as Harold Napoleon) have come to similar conclusions even though they were completely unaware of Handsome Lake.

The basic theory underlying this method is that Native cultures are under attack and many Native people are alienated from their heritage. These conditions can cause people to experience stress that triggers substance abuse. By strengthening the culture and developing a good relationship with it, however, people can develop the tools they need to recovery.

Chapter 2 provides an overview of the Handsome Lake program that consists of the Path of Handsome Lake (a series of steps to follow toward recovery) and the Landmarks of the Path (a series of useful ways to achieve the goals of the steps).

Having provided a somewhat theoretic overview in chapter 2, chapters 3 and 4 deal with practical matters the therapist needs to apply the method. Chapter 3 provides a general overview of therapy that uses the method. Chapter 4 continues with a more "nuts and bolts" discussion that provides a number of practical tips and suggestions.

It is hoped that these chapters will provide the therapist with the orientation they need to apply the program.

Chapter 2

The Handsome Lake Method

An Introduction[1]

DIVERSITY AND RECOVERY

Increasingly, substance abuse counselors recognize that cultural issues impact both dysfunction and recovery. This realization follows decades in which differences between people were ignored or discounted. The Twelve Steps Program of Alcoholics Anonymous and Narcotics Anonymous, for example, tends to link substance abuse with a spiritual bankruptcy that can affect people from all cultures and ways of life. Such a vision minimizes the differences between people and focus on their similarities (dysfunctional tendencies triggered by substance abuse.)

Currently, in contrast, the differences between people are being recognized. Thus, the Secular Organization for Recovery (SOS) offers a secular alternative to what is perceived as the religious and spiritual ethos of Alcoholics Anonymous/the Twelve Steps method (Christopher, 1992, 1997). Rational Recovery (Trimpey, 1985) and Self Management and Recovery Training (Hovarth, 1997), also offer nonspiritual and rational alternatives of therapy and self-help.

Other organizations, such as Women for Sobriety (Kirkpatrick, 1978, 1990), tailor themselves around the needs of women, arguing that females, as a group, have a series of special needs and vulnerabilities (that revolve around self-esteem, guilt, etc.) In all of these cases, a universal program of recovery (typified by

Alcoholics Anonymous/the Twelve Steps method) is rejected and replaced by techniques that are tailored toward the needs of specific groups.

Cultural differences also need to be addressed. I have been told, for example, that many Hispanic men embrace a "macho" posture and, as a result, they may have trouble admitting to any kind of "powerlessness," even though doing so is a keystone of the Alcoholics Anonymous/Twelve Steps program. Some Native Americans, furthermore, are rather private and reserved and may not be comfortable discussing their misdeeds (or even their positive achievements) within the context of an open forum (as encouraged by the Twelve Steps program.) And since the Twelve Steps method is the brainchild of middle class White men, various groups complain that the approach is not well suited to them. Thus, a number of African Americans have confided to me that they can embrace Alcoholics Anonymous only with difficulty and that much of the rhetoric they hear at meetings is not relevant to them, as members of the Black community. I have heard numerous Native people make similar observations.

Today, universal strategies of recovery are being replaced with an emphasis on diversity. Currently, Lance Dodes (2002) and Stanton Peele (1992) have emerged as particularly vocal critics of Alcoholics

Anonymous arguing that substance abusers need methods that help reduce the stress that can trigger dysfunction.

NATIVE AMERICANS AND ALCOHOL/ SUBSTANCE ABUSE

Today, there is a recognition that Native people experience a distinct series of vulnerabilities and needs that can trigger dysfunction. As mentioned above, many Native Americans are not well served by universal strategies of treatment, such as those associated with the Twelve Steps program.

Cultural differences appear to contribute to the tendency toward ineffectiveness. This situation is multiplied by the fact that Native Americans in general, consist of a heterogeneous group of diverse cultures, societies, and nations that cannot all be conveniently lumped together (any more than various White cultures—such as the German, English, Italian, and Irish—that are distinctive and need to be accepted as such.) In addition, since some Native Americans live in a reservation setting while others reside within the larger community, different individuals face a varied pressures. As a result, no one strategy of recovery is likely to be universally applicable to all Native Americans.

An appropriate method (or metaphor) for promoting recovery among Native Americans is sorely needed. This technique must be able to transcend the differences that exist between a wide range of Native cultures, while mitigating the socioeconomic pressures that Natives collectively face. Among these impacts are (1) profound encroachments by the dominant culture, (2) economic hardship, (3) the generally reduced status of Native Americans within the mainstream world, (4) being subjected to a ubiquitous process of cultural genocide/the conflict of being caught between worlds, and (5) the relentless undercutting of the cultural traditions that usually bind people together and provide meaning and significance to life.

Therapists and clients often attempt to meld a program of recovery with aspects of the traditional culture. Although recognizing that all cultures can and should evolve and that individual people need to respond to circumstance, counselors and clients should not forget the negative power of unmitigated social change. Both therapists and clients, furthermore, need to recognize that cultures, although evolving, can maintain themselves and continue to function. This is true, even though specific individuals simultaneously have a niche in both the mainstream world and in traditional culture. It is equally vital to remember that when individuals have a niche and a stake in two different (and potentially competing) communities, conflict and stress are likely to develop.

Encouragingly, cultures often respond to challenges in a positive and constructive way, and continue to be a powerful force in people's lives. By recognizing that mental health tends to be nurtured by a strong cultural underpinning, both therapists and clients are reminded of the role that a person's heritage and traditions play in promoting good mental health.

This book deals with that reality by using the example and tools of a nineteenth century Iroquois leader, Handsome Lake, a man who overcame alcoholism while simultaneously helping his culture to adjust to changing times—and, thereby, revitalize itself.

THE CALDRON OF HANDSOME LAKE

The Iroquois of New York State and Ontario, Cananda are (and long have been) an impressive people and a powerful and proud nation. Without the aid of White leadership, the Iroquois created a complex government; some observers even suggest that documents like the Declaration of Independence and the United States' Constitution were influenced by the example of the Iroquois. If makes no difference if these speculations are fact or legend; in any event, the Iroquois are a complicated nation that has achieved greatness and deserves our respect. The fact that the Iroquois have suffered hard times in recent centuries does not cast a shadow on these achievements.

In the colonial era, the British and the French were competing for control of what is now Ontario, Canada and western New York. Up through and including the French and Indian War, the Iroquois were able to manipulate the situation and enjoy the prosperity that resulted. Good things, unfortunately, do not last forever:

> With the victory of the British in the War with France the Iroquois found themselves outflanked, no longer able to play off the British and French against each other and surrounded by a circle of British forts. (Wallace, p. 442)

When White military leaders no longer needed their Native allies, the situation of the Iroquois declined and the generosity of the British dwindled.

When the Revolutionary War began, the Iroquois again became embroiled in a conflict that was larger than their world. Being caught in the middle (since much of the fighting took place on Iroquois territory), they had to decide which side to support. Realizing that the British wanted Iroquois territory merely for trading purposes and fearing that many Whites would migrate into Iroquois land if the revolution were successful, most Iroquois sided with Britain.[2]

Although the decision to ally with the British was a reasonable choice, it was costly:

> [During the war, the Iroquois homeland] was devastated by the John Sullivan [United States military commander] expedition in 1778, which in a three-pronged offensive managed to burn the houses and the crops in almost every major Iroquois town. Many of the women and children, and the surviving warriors, took refuge at Fort Niagara with the British, who housed them in a refugee camp, inadequately clothed, inadequately fed, inadequately sheltered, and swept by disease. By the end of the war, despite their military successes, the Iroquois population had been cut approximately in half. (Wallace, p. 443)

The war took a terrible toll on the Iroquois, both in the cost of human lives and when viewed in political and economic terms.

After the war, the victorious United States, remembering that the Iroquois had been their enemies in the battle for independence, showed them few favors. As the Iroquois leaders had predicted, furthermore, hordes of White settlers were attracted the area. By the turn of the nineteenth century the Iroquois were beaten in war, decimated by diseases brought by the Whites, and besieged by social and economic rivals. The results of this unenviable situation include infighting, personal resignation, and retreat. As is often the case under such circumstances, dysfunctional behavior (including alcoholism) became rampant.

Noted anthropologist, Anthony Wallace observes that many examples of what therapists and psychiatrists recognize as pathological behavior existed; they include rampant violence, uncontrolled weeping and pining, fear of peers (as evidenced by accusations of witchcraft), social disunity, and, widespread alcoholism. Clinical depression was commonplace and Wallace observes that when people were sober, they were likely to be suicidal (1970, 196-201).

ANOMIE: THE PAIN OF SOCIAL AND CULTURAL DISRUPTION

Looking at the situation faced by the Iroquois of the late eighteenth/early nineteenth century, the telltale signs of traumatic social change and cultural disintegration are obvious. These processes, in turn, went hand in hand with an epidemic of alcoholism. Handsome Lake, a forceful Iroquois leader, provides a classic example of that syndrome as well as a demonstration of how the cultural heritage of a people can be instrumental in recovery. The case of Handsome Lake and the Iroquois, furthermore, are hardly exceptions to the rule; indeed, the sociological concept of anomie has long dealt with the disruption and pain caused by social change. It is useful, therefore, to discuss the process of anomie, as distilled by social theorists such as Robert Merton, before dealing with Handsome Lake as a specific example of alienation/alcoholism and readjustment/recovery.

Discussed in layman's terms, anomie has sometimes been equated with "normlessness," although a more theoretical definition indicates that it:

> signifies the state of mind of one who ... has no longer any sense of continuity, of folk, of obligation. The anomic man has become spiritually sterile, responsive only to himself, responsible to no one. (MacIver, 1950, p. 84)

As a result, individuals who experience anomie become alienated and cut off from their heritage. As Dressler observes:

To put it allegorically, the anomic individual has lost his past, foresees no future and lives only in the immediate which is virtually nowhere. (Dressler, 1969, p. 251)

According to Robert Merton, a major twentieth century social theorist, a key cause and source of anomie is a disparity between the goals that society gives to people and the means of achieving them; when this unhealthy situation arises, anomie is the likely result (Merton, 1957, pp. 121-194). Specifically, Merton argues that the mores and norms of a society provide its members with goals to which they should aspire, on the one hand, and socially acceptable methods for achieving these goals, on the other. Over time, however, the culture (or the socioeconomic milieu in which it exists) may change to such a degree that its members are no longer able to achieve sanctioned and honored goals in a socially acceptable manner. It goes without saying that the plight of the Iroquois in the late eighteenth/early nineteenth century placed them in such a situation.

Merton went on to suggest that when people cannot achieve their goals in socially acceptable ways, the propensity for deviant behavior increases. Thus, mainstream upper middle class people (who have a relatively good chance of achieving their goals in socially acceptable ways) tend to act in accordance with cultural norms, even though some may resort to "white collar crime." Those in less fortunate circumstances, in contrast, are more likely to embrace some sort of deviant response. Members of minority groups and those who are members of cultures that are out of step with the dominant hierarchy (such as Native people who largely embrace their traditional heritage and/or have not mastered "mainstream ways") are particularly likely to act in deviant and/or dysfunctional ways. That was the precise response exhibited by many Iroquois in the late eighteenth/early nineteenth centuries. Many Native people from throughout the world are currently responding in a parallel manner.

The concept of anomie continues to be a useful concept. Representative applications of the concept have been used to explain the formation of teenage gangs (Cloward & Ohlin, 1960; Jankowski, 1991), to explore deviance in seventeenth century Puritan society (Erikson, 1966), and to explain "moral panics" in contemporary Great Britian (Jenkins, 1992). The concept of anomie is one of the keystone theories of social change and deviant behavior and it tends to be commonly used in research that deals with these phenomena. In addition, the concept of anomie has been used to describe the plight of people who, like many Native Americans, are members of hinterland or ethnic/cultural enclaves.

Nonetheless, a cultural heritage typically has the ability to serve, protect, and nurture individuals. As Walle has observed when discussing the impact of economic development upon such populations:

Ultimately, culture helps people cope with the stresses of "future shock" and rapid social and economic transformations.… [By adopting] a social structural approach … [it is possible to be aware] that changes in one area of a culture typically trigger other transformations which may be both unanticipated and negative. [A strong traditional culture can mitigate these impacts]. (Walle, 1998, pp. 182-183)

Thus, while individuals may suffer from anomie due to circumstances that are beyond their control, a strong and vital cultural tradition can help to mitigate these negative forces. If the culture is weakened and not functioning in a coherent way, however, it will lose its ability to help people cope with the struggles and challenges they face.

In situations where cultural traditions have been significantly undercut and/or where they are unable to help their members to cope with the problems faced, individuals may begin to act in counterproductive ways. Of special interest to us here is Merton's category of "retreatism" that he presents as one response to anomie. Merton observes that retreatism occurs among people who embrace both the goals of society and the proscribed methods of achieving them, but are unable to succeed in socially accepted ways. Merton suggests that retreatists include hermits, the mentally ill, and *alcoholics, and drug abusers.*

Thus, when the culture (or the circumstances within which the culture operates) no longer provides an appropriate avenue for personal achievement and self-respect, the result is likely to be retreatism, a response that often plays itself out in substance abuse.

Many Native Americans appear to be locked into this hurtful situation societies. The inability of these people to succeed in ways that reflect their traditional culture leads some Native Americans to retreat from society. Drug and alcohol abuse are specific types of retreat. As a result, some substance abuse among Native Americans can be viewed as a response to anomie caused by stresses upon or a breakdown of the traditional culture.

As is common knowledge, many Native Americans have experienced a profound breakdown in their traditional cultures and, on many occasions, no alternative has emerged to fill the void. This is exactly the kind of situation where anomie is predicted to develop and where retreatist responses are likely to lead to substance abuse. Such perspectives coincide with current trends in substance abuse therapy that see a connection between feelings of helplessness and a tendency towards dysfunction. Thus, Lance Dodes, best known for his *Heart of Addiction* states:

> Virtually every addictive act is preceded by a feeling of helplessness or powerlessness. Addictive behavior functions to [mitigate the] … underlying feeling of helplessness.

In presenting this point, Dodes emphasizes that working to eliminate feelings of helplessness is the key to recovery. Stanton Peele (1992), mirroring Dodes, notes that alcoholics often describe their addiction as a form of "self-medication" that helps them to cope with the pressures of life. Peele, as Dodes, believes that substance abuse is a way of dealing with situational stress and tension.

As can be seen, the concept of anomie deals with the impacts of social change and the disruptions that it causes in people's lives. One specific response to the pressures of anomie is retreatism (withdrawing from the world). According to Merton, alcohol abuse is often a form of retreatism that can be explained as a response to anomie. Many Native Americans who suffer from alcoholism appear to have fallen victim to this kind of counterproductive response to social change and alienation.

THE RECOVERY CONTINUUM OF HANDSOME LAKE: AN OVERVIEW

The story of Handsome Lake is a saga of cultural decay that led to dysfunction and alcoholism, on the one hand, and a return to sobriety and cultural rebirth, on the other. By examining these two different aspects of the Handsome Lake story, it is possible to make some useful observations about anomie and alcoholism and relate them to the circumstances faced by contemporary Native people.

The story takes place among the Iroquois of the late eighteenth/early nineteenth century, a society that, as described above, had suffered grievously due to defeat, disease, cultural disruption, and social change. Because of their situation, the Iroquois suffered from the pain of anomie and they responded in typical ways including a high incidence of dysfunctional behavior. In specific, alcoholism ran rampant.

Within this setting of defeat and despair, Handsome Lake, a once respected member of Iroquois society, had fallen into the abyss of ungoverned alcoholism. Out of control and seriously ill, it appeared that his productive life was over. By the spring of 1799, his drinking and its impacts had grown steadily worse:

> Handsome Lake … was bedridden, reputedly … as a consequence of prolonged alcoholic access. (Wallace, 1978, p. 445).

In the June of that year:

> Handsome Lake collapsed … in the presence of his daughter … he appeared to have died, but actually he was in a trance state and was experiencing the first of a series of visions in which messengers of the Creator instructed him in his own and his people's religious obligations. (Wallace, pp. 445)

After his recuperation from apparent death, Handsome Lake emerged as a new man, and one who dedicated his life to personal sobriety and to the cultural rebirth of Iroquois society.

Eventually these visions (and Handsome Lake's insights regarding them), were synthesized into a new strategy by which the Iroquois (both as a culture and as specific individuals) could stem their decline.

On the one hand, Handsome Lake encouraged his people to embrace their cultural traditions. The late eighteenth and early nineteenth century had devastated the Iroquois and their culture was in a state of complete disarray. In the midst of this chaos, Handsome Lake forcefully championed his culture, its traditions, and the nobility and worth of the Iroquois heritage.

This embrace and championing of Iroquois culture, however, was not merely envisioned as paying homage to the past. Handsome Lake clearly recognized that if Iroquois society was to be revitalized it would have to transform itself in line with the realities of contemporary life. Thus, Iroquois men had long been hunters and warriors and they left farming to women, viewing it as an unmanly and shameful profession. When White people migrated into Iroquois territory, however, new methods of farming (that included men performing their share of the work) began to outstrip Iroquois farming techniques. As a result, these newcomers further undercut the Iroquois economy. Under these circumstances, Handsome Lake encouraged Iroquois men to take up farming and he urged them to perceive agriculture as a legitimate profession that should not be a source of shame or embarrassment.

In his discussions of anomie, Robert Merton has pointed to "innovation" as one possible response to an environment in which people cannot achieve their goals in socially acceptable ways. It must be noted, however, that Merton was referring to a relatively stable culture and, therefore, he depicts innovation as an illegitimate means of success (such as criminal behavior.) Antisocial or not, embracing the innovation may provide better opportunities for success and, therefore, can help to eliminate the ravages of anomie.

In the case of Handsome Lake, he took illegitimate behaviors (men farming, as a prime example) and transformed them into acceptable and honorable pursuits. As a result of the innovations that Handsome Lake advocated, Iroquois society found itself in a better position to respond to the circumstances faced in the early nineteenth century. It is easy to see the value of Handsome Lake's solution; he offered an alternative to cultural decline and poverty. Providing an option to retreatist responses (such as alcoholism), Handsome Lake offered an innovative alternative

that led to a positive cultural rebirth and a firmer economic foundation for Iroquois society.

Handsome Lake coupled the embrace of traditional Iroquois culture (albeit adjusted to circumstance) with an insistence that people cease pursuing activities that were disruptive and dysfunctional. Drinking alcoholic beverages was high on the list of banned behaviors.[3] Being an alcoholic himself, Handsome Lake was well aware of the dangers of alcohol and he strongly discouraged the use of alcoholic beverages. Although Handsome Lake's position is more extreme than that of Alcoholics Anonymous (since Alcoholics Anonymous sees no reason for successful social drinkers to abstain), this response seems to be closely akin to the American temperance movement that was taking root during the nineteenth century and which ultimately flowered into the legalized prohibition movement of the early twentieth century. In addition, Mormonism (another highly successful religion that emerged at approximately the same time and the same location as that of Handsome Lake)[4] places a similar ban on alcoholic beverages. Apparently both White and Native American reformers from Western New York in the early nineteenth century were aware of the devastating impact of alcohol on both individuals and society; as a result, they urged tight controls.

Having embraced and updated his cultural traditions and choosing to abstain from dysfunctional activities, including alcoholic drinking, Handsome Lake insisted that people acknowledge their past errors, sins, and wayward ways in order to refrain from similar misdeeds in the future.

Largely through the example and the message of Handsome Lake, the Iroquois people were able to stem their downward spiral of decline and to re-emerge as a vital cultural entity. As a result, many Iroquois who had suffered from alcoholic behavior were able to enjoy what we now call "recovery" (reclaiming their lives through spiritual growth coupled with abstinence.)

This, in a nutshell, is the history of the heritage and legacy of Handsome Lake. His story is recorded in various places[5] and the reader is encouraged to consult both primary and secondary sources for more details about his life, his bout with alcoholism, the accomplishments after his recovery, and the revitalization of Iroquois society that resulted from his leadership.

THE PATH OF HANDSOME LAKE

Having provided an historic overview of the life and contribution of Handsome Lake, it becomes necessary to distill his vision and his achievements into a useable set of principles that are appropriate for therapy. The model I have distilled will be called the "Path of Handsome Lake." Although the words used are not precisely those of Handsome Lake, the basic message and the way in which it is presented clearly reflect his vision. They form a suggested program of therapy that stems from one of the most revered and influential Native American reformers.

This path, as suggested by Handsome Lake, consists of six components that combine cultural health with individual well-being. It stresses that dysfunction and alcoholism can be overcome by simultaneously focusing on both cultural and individual concerns. Not only were Handsome Lake's methods effective among the nineteenth century Iroquois, they provide a means of combating dysfunction in today's world. The suggested "Path of Handsome Lake" includes:

1. *Embrace tradition*: "I possess a culture and a tradition. Embracing them is sacred, meaningful, and joyful."
2. *Transform your tradition to keep it strong*: "All cultural traditions change and all cultural traditions are under attack. I will strive to help my culture evolve and flourish."
3. *Stop alcohol/substance abuse*: "I will break the cycle of personal and cultural decay by ceasing to abuse alcohol."
4. *Admit to errors made*: "I recognize my past errors and I will remember them when choosing a more noble and fulfilling path."
5. *Do not repeat errors of the past*: "Having chosen a more noble and fulfilling path, I will strive to keep my errors in the past and correct them as soon as they occur."
6. *Heritage and recovery*. "My heritage and my traditions give me a spirituality. By ignoring my heritage and my traditions, I am denying my own

self and I may become vulnerable to relapse. By embracing, my heritage, I can better succeed in recovery and in life."

As a useful device, I have culled a six-fold path from the teachings of Handsome Lake in order to affirm how he combined a concern for a healthy society with strategies designed to overcome personal dysfunction. This process goes hand in hand with strengthening and nourishing the cultural, its heritage, and traditions.

COMPARING THE PATH OF HANDSOME LAKE AND ALCOHOLICS ANONYMOUS

In many ways, the Path of Handsome Lake and the Twelve Steps of Alcoholics Anonymous are parallel. Indeed, these two programs of recovery are in general agreement in many ways. Alcoholics Anonymous, however, does not deal with various issues that are of concern to Native people who are faced with profound cultural stress and disruption. This void seems to be the result of the fact that Alcoholics Anonymous was the product of relatively successful (aside from their alcoholism) middle class White men who were firmly a part of the dominant culture of their era. These individuals, as a group, do not appear to have been victimized by the impact of rampant social/cultural change and anomie (even though they lived through the Depression). Thus, Alcoholics Anonymous was not formed by people who were likely to be suffering from anomie and it does not dwell on the specific issues that impact people who are the victims of the kind of circumstances that triggers retreatism.

Alcoholics Anonymous, however, is not inherently at odds with using the Path of Handsome Lake as a tool of recovery. As a result, although Native people who are suffering from alcoholism can clearly benefit from Alcoholics Anonymous, they may need to devote supplemental attention to the fact that their cultures are under profound attack from pressures that are beyond their control.

Table 2.1 compares the Path of Handsome Lake method with those of Alcoholics Anonymous and the Twelve Steps program

THE LANDMARKS AND THEIR PURPOSE

While the Path of Handsome Lake links personal recovery to cultural health, the Landmarks of the Path introduces more concrete goals and specific targets of action. While the Landmarks do not replace the Path, they provide a method of following its guidelines.

As with the Path of Handsome Lake, the Landmarks of the Path can be presented as a six-step process. These steps include:

1. "We recognize who we are."
2. "We acknowledge that our heritage, culture, and traditions are our strength."
3. "We reject the vulnerability that comes from ignoring our roots."
4. "We realize that others may have their own traditions and we respect them."
5. "We understand that strength that comes from embracing ourselves, not retreating from challenges."
6. "Handsome Lake's example and advice may be useful to all who face personal disruptions."

In this manner, the Landmarks provide a systematic way of addressing the needs of Natives whose drift into substance abuse may be the result of an alienation from their heritage. Each will be briefly discussed.

1.   WE RECOGNIZE WHO WE ARE

In general, progress results when people recognize who they are and act accordingly. People, however, are very complex and are made up of many bits of personality, character, and past experience. Some of these categories may include negative traits (such as a personal vulnerability to substance abuse). People are both individuals and part of a heritage or culture. And they may be torn between different goals, motives, and rival cultural traditions. These are issues that need to be confronted in a positive and constructive way. Native people are often strongly influenced by their cultural origins, even if they are not aware of it. As a result, it is important for Native people to consider the importance of their cultural heritage and think in terms of it.

As people seek recovery, they need to understand who they are. By possessing this vision of their identity, the influences impacting them, and their potentials for the future, people are better able to meet the challenges of life. And overcoming substance abuse is one of the greatest battles anybody will ever fight.

2.   WE ACKNOWLEDGE THAT OUR HERITAGE, CULTURE, AND TRADITIONS ARE OUR STRENGTH

Not only do people need to understand who they are and the fact that their Native heritage is a big part of their identity, they also need to recognize that their ethnic identity can give them strength, power, and purpose. A strong and positive cultural connection is a powerful asset even if it is often ignored. Forgetting a cultural identity and thinking it has little effect can prove to be very hurtful.

Those who recognize their cultural identity can avoid be blindsided by failing to understand how their culture is part of them and how it impacts the way they think, feel, and behave.

3.   WE REJECT THE VULNERABILITY THAT COMES FROM IGNORING OUR ROOTS

As Native cultures have been drawn into the mainstream world, there has been a tendency for people to ignore their roots. When this happens, Native people are likely to deny their cultural heritage and experience alienation, pain, and sorrow. Doing so can trigger dysfunctional behavior, such as substance abuse. Developing an awareness of their cultural traditions and making them a more conscious part of their lives can be important tools of recovery.

Having recognized the power and importance of their heritage, the value of self-reflection becomes all the more obvious. By rejecting the vulnerability that comes from ignoring their heritage, people can make progress.

4.   WE REALIZE THAT OTHERS MAY HAVE THEIR OWN TRADITIONS AND WE RESPECT THEM

Cultural traditions touch people in very personal ways. As a result, those from different cultures are apt to experience their own feelings, motives, goals, strengths, and weaknesses. Nonetheless, people who

Table 2.1.
The Path of Handsome Lake and Alcoholics Anonymous Compared

Path	Discussion	Compared With AA
1. *Embrace tradition*: "I possess a culture and a tradition. Embracing them is sacred, meaningful, and joyful."	People often need to be reminded that they are members of social and cultural traditions that profoundly impact them in both overt and covert ways.	The founders of AA did not think in terms of specific cultural traditions and envisioned their program as universal. They however, did not rule out other programs.
2. *Help keep traditions strong*: "All cultural traditions change and are under attack. I will strive to help my culture evolve and flourish."	Helps people to understand how cultures may be under attack and that both individuals and the collective society should work to strengthen cultural ties.	The founders of AA do not think in terms of cultural stress, the fact that cultures evolve, or the impact of social stress upon alcoholic behavior.
3. *Stop alcohol/substance abuse*: "I will break the cycle of personal and cultural decay by ceasing substance abuse."	It is vital to deal with both the individual and the cultural impacts of substance abuse. While substance abuse is an individual disease, it also has cultural causes and implications	AA embraces the disease concept of alcoholism and emphasized that to successfully restructure their lives, total abstinence is essential. The impact of substance abuse upon others is recognized
4. *Admit to errors made*: "I recognize my past errors and I will remember them when choosing a more noble and fulfilling path."	Under the influence of substance abuse, many individuals act in shameful, careless, or hurtful ways. It is necessary to acknowledge this potential and make amends as appropriate.	Steps 4 through 9 of the 12 Steps of AA specifically deal with recognizing the errors of the past and atoning for them.
5. *Do not repeat errors of the past;* "Having chosen a more noble and fulfilling path, I will strive to keep my errors in the past and correct them as soon as they occur."	Developing a pattern of appropriate and noble behavior is essential for both the health of the culture, the recovering individual, and the people with whom the recovering individual interacts.	Step 10 of the 12 Steps of AA recommends that people maintain a vigilant guard against error and to immediately atone for errors when they do occur.
6. *Heritage and recovery.* "My heritage and my traditions give me a spirituality. By denying them, I deny my own self and I may become vulnerable to relapse. By embracing, them, I can better succeed in recovery and in life."	The concept of anomie suggests that personal alienation and/or cultural decay can lead to substance abuse. As a result, recovering people will be less prone to relapse if their culture is a powerful force that is able to provide them with support.	The founders of AA did not specifically deal with the impact of the larger culture upon the health of the individual recovering person.
Discussion	The Path of Handsome Lake and the methods of Alcoholics Anonymous and its 12 Step Program dovetail and do not conflict with one another. The Path of Handsome Lake, however, is better able to deal with the impact of cultural stress upon substance abuse and the need for people to be attuned to their cultural traditions.	

band together in search of recovery often come from different backgrounds. This is true in the mainstream world as well in programs of recovery that are geared around the special needs of Native people. Even specific Native traditions (such as the Athabascan, people of Alaska) are made up of many subgroups that are distinct from each other in significant ways. It is important to develop an appreciation of (and if necessary a tolerance for) other peoples and their way of life. Various programs of recovery attempt, in their own way, to deal with the fact that people band together to combat substance abuse.

People are products of their own heritage; it provides them with a distinct way of being human. Other people, in contrast, have their own traditions. Learning about, acknowledging, and celebrating diversity is important and empowering. It is also essential if different people are to work together for their common well being.

5.   WE UNDERSTAND THAT STRENGTH COMES FROM EMBRACING OURSELVES, NOT RETREATING FROM CHALLENGES

If people are to put their lives in order, they need to accept themselves for who they are. A part of this identity involves the degree to which Native people fit into the mainstream culture. While the larger world (and people's place within it) may need to be acknowledged and embraced, this represents only a part of personal identity. Aspects of the mainstream world, however, are often more obvious to people than their traditional cultural heritage.

Rapid change takes a hurtful toll. I am reminded of the term "future shock" that was coined by Alvin Toffler many years ago. Toffler noted that modern society is in such a rapid state of change that people, raised in one era, must live in world that has quickly become profoundly different. As a result, people become alienated. Toffler, of course, was inspired by the anthropological idea of "culture shock" in which people entering a foreign society often face stress, confusion, and dysfunction. Native people, of course, are often simultaneously impacted by both future shock and culture shock. Their world is changing quickly and their cultures are often being overpowered by alien ways of life. It should come as little surprise that

many Native people exposed to these pressures suffer from substance abuse and other dysfunctions.

By re-embracing their traditions, people can gain the strength they need to meet the problems of life. By understanding and accepting who they are, people can better employ the tools that their culture provides and use them to combat their problems.

Those suffering from substance abuse often drink and drug in order to retreat from the challenges they face. On many occasions, Native people are confronted by crises linked to the fact that their cultures are in a state of disarray and/or because they are not adequately attuned with their heritage. An antidote for these problems is to for people to accept their cultural heritage and work to embrace and strengthen it.

6.   HANDSOME LAKE'S EXAMPLE MAY BE USEFUL TO OTHERS WHO FACE PERSONAL DISRUPTIONS

Programs of recovery typically point to the value of helping others. When people are given a second chance in life, they often want to share their good fortune. While they should do so in a nonforceful and nonjudgmental manner, helping others is beneficial both to the giver and the receiver.

This program is built on developing personal and cultural self-awareness. It suggests that if people better understand who they are and why they respond in the way they do they can better cope with their the pressures of life.

Handsome Lake challenges people to live a sober and moral life. He also emphasizes that this goal can best be achieved when people develop an awareness of, culturally, who they are. Native substance abusers seeking recovery can benefit from Handsome Lake's example and the advice he gives. All people, furthermore, can benefit from acknowledging who they are and by using that reality as a stepping stone toward recovery.

By embracing their cultural heritage and by understanding its impact, recovering substance abusers can gain valuable tools of sobriety. By ignoring their traditions, in contrast, profound triggers to dysfunctional behavior can easily remain unaddressed and sources of strength may remain untapped. The Landmarks are presented in Table 2.2.

Viewed in this way, the Landmarks of the Path emerges as a specific set of strategies that people can employ to rebuild their heritage, affirm their connection to it, and live a productive and fruitful life as they recover from substance abuse. While the Landmarks is not the Path suggested by Handsome Lake, it does provide clues, suggestions, and orientations on how to follow it.

HANDSOME LAKE AND RECOVERY

This book views the example of Handsome Lake as a model of recovery for Native people. Handsome Lake personally dealt with issues concerning the decay and rebirth of cultural traditions and their impact on substance abuse (and other dysfunctional behaviors.) He developed a strategy of recovery centered on cultural issues that transcends, while not totally eclipsing,

Table 2.2.   Landmarks of the Path

Landmark	Significance	Discussion
Recognize who we are	People in recovery need to understand their strengths, weaknesses, and identities.	Although AA's Twelve Steps program focuses on strengths and weaknesses, it does not deal with cultural identities.
Acknowledge power of culture	Recovering people often need to acknowledge their cultural identity and what it impacts.	If people are unaware of their cultural identity, they might not totally understand themselves.
Transcend alienation	When cultures are weakened or ignored, people can become vulnerable to substance abuse. By strengthening these traditions, dysfunction can be attacked	The dysfunctional behavior resulting form alienation can be reversed by strengthening and embracing the culture.
Respect other traditions	Other people possess cultures and traditions that are meaningful to them. These heritages deserve the respect of others.	Recovery often takes place alongside those from different cultures. Understanding and honoring different cultures are important.
Embrace ourselves	Since cultural identity is a crucial part of personality and character, people need to become consciously aware of it and its power.	By better understanding their personality, character, and cultural origins, substance abusers can better restructure their lives and recover.
Many can benefit	Because ignoring a cultural identity potentially impacts all people, those from many different cultures can benefit from following the Path of Handsome Lake.	Many people, some more than others, have suffered grievous impacts from rapid cultural change. They can benefit from this program.
Discussion	The Landmarks of the Path provides a means of applying the Path of Handsome Lake. It can also be used to gauge the degree to which progress is being made. It focuses the power and significance of the cultural heritage and it seeks to unite people of different traditions while acknowledging their distinctiveness.	

other therapeutic methods. By taking cues directly from the life and teachings of Handsome Lake, a method tailored around the needs of Native substance abusers who have been impacted by social disruption and anomie is proposed.

Predating, but in complete agreement with modern theories of sociology such as anomie, Handsome Lake recognized the impact of cultural stress on dysfunction. Aware of this connection, Handsome Lake understood that the recovery of the individual and the viability of society go hand in hand. Given this reality, he affirmed that cultures should embrace their traditions and heritage while adjusting them to mesh with existing circumstances. By combining sobriety with appropriate cultural and personal strategies, he provided a path to recovery.

Essentially Handsome Lake:

1. Recognized that pain and suffering are caused by profound and unmitigated social change;
2. Advocated preserving traditions, on the one hand, while updating them to they can function effectively, on the other; and
3. Linked recovery to cultural strength coupled with individual effort.

These perspectives dovetail with many of the components of the Twelve Steps program of Alcoholics Anonymous and Narcotics Anonymous that urge personal responsibility, penance, and ongoing vigilance. Embracing these principles expands beyond generic programs of recovery by dealing with cultural issues.

GUIDELINES FOR COUNSELORS AND THERAPISTS

A basic premise of this book is that generalized programs of recovery (such as Alcoholics Anonymous/ Narcotics Anonymous and the Twelve Steps method) are currently being augmented by specialized alternatives that deal with the specific needs of specific people. Among Native people, alternatives are sorely needed because mainstream, generic programs like Alcoholics Anonymous/Narcotics Anonymous were created without any specific reference to the impact of massive cultural stress and its hurtful impact on people.

The Handsome Lake method deals with these cultural issues by expanding beyond generic programs, on the one hand, while simultaneously dealing with profound and often disabling impacts of social change, on the other. The resulting self-help strategy can be fruitfully employed by Native people who seek to recover from substance abuse.

A benefit of this program is that it acknowledges the impact of social stress while helping people to (1) cope with these pressures and (2) restructure themselves and their cultures in order to deal with the challenges that are faced. Because the founders of the Twelve Steps program were members of the dominant culture of their era, they do not deal in a forceful manner with cultural stress and disintegration. As a result, although the Twelve Steps program is useful, it does not provide a full answer to substance abusers whose cultures are experiencing profound stress, decay, and disruption.

Handsome Lake, in contrast, clearly understood how cultural stress can trigger dysfunctional behavior. As a result, his work and example suggest a self-help program that can be linked to cultural renewal. Because many indigenous people face cultural stress, they will benefit from a program that recognizes and responds to these pressures.

BEYOND NATIVE AMERICANS

While Native Americans are distinct in many ways from other Native and traditional people, the stress and pressures exerted on their cultures are mirrored by the experiences of many other ethnic enclaves that are confronted by the outside world. Thus, Harold Napoleon (1996), a Yup'ik (Native Alaskan ethnic group) has noted the hurtful impacts of cultural decline and he has independently suggested strategies of recovery that parallel the suggestions of Handsome Lake. Although these two Native leaders lives 200 years apart and worked independently of each other, the similarities between them represent independent inventions that have been triggered by parallel conditions.

Among Native Hawaiians and the Maori of New Zealand, furthermore, profound similarities also exist. Thus, as Salzman (2001) emphasizes:

Old Hawaiian customs, previously bonded together by ancient Polynesian beliefs, now fractured by the overthrow of the traditional religion were collapsing at all levels. As a result of the understandably bewilderment, Hawaiians plunged to a new low. (p. 177)

The responses of Native Hawaiians to this trauma also parallel those of the Iroquois. Unprecedented stress resulted in a breakdown of society. Cultural disintegration, however, is currently being mitigated by an embrace and revitalization of the Native culture, on the one hand, while adjusting it to prevailing/ unavoidable conditions on the other. As a result, a pattern of substance abuse and eventual recovery that is similar to that exhibited by the Iroquois has been noted.

The parallels between the nineteenth century Iroquois and the Maori of New Zealand are even more striking. As Gilgen (1996) observes:

There are many similarities between (Native American and Maori) experiences.... A disproportionate over-representation in the prisons, abhorrent statistics regarding disease and health issues, dismal failure of the educations al system, and the highest ratio of unemployed people in the country. (p. 52)

Gilgen continues:

My ancestors were traumatized by a great death, a period in which Maori culture was attacked physically, spiritually, and culturally through disease, land confiscation, inter-tribal warfare, and the introduction of alcohol and non-indigenous religions. To deal with the rape of our land and culture, we also used a range of coping mechanisms that included self-blame, alcohol abuse, violence among ourselves, depression, suicide, and denial. (p. 52)

These conditions and responses, of course, closely resemble the situation of the nineteenth century Iroquois. The independently invented means of overcoming such circumstances, furthermore, was a form of cultural renewal that parallels the suggestions of Handsome Lake.

Native people throughout the world need to recognize that, although they come from different cultural traditions, many individuals and Native societies are unified by negative impacts triggered by the domi-nant culture. The ways in which Native people have responded to these challenges, furthermore, have tended to include inappropriate and counterproductive responses (such as substance abuse.)

Different Native peoples can learn from each other regarding how to cope with the impacts of the outside world. In doing so, they can combine their experiences in order to formulate appropriate coping mechanisms and strategies of recovery. As a first step in this important process, the example of Handsome Lake's leadership among the nineteenth century Iroquois demonstrates how cultural renewal and personal recovery can coincide with each other.

It is hoped that the example of Handsome Lake will encourage substance abuse counselors who deal with Native people (as well as the clients themselves) to more effectively deal with the issue of cultural stress and its impact on substance abuse.

APPENDIX: A NOTE ON HANDSOME LAKE'S PARTISAN NATURE AND ITS IMPLICATION

While recalling the recovery of Handsome Lake and using it as a metaphor is useful, remembering that his life and his work also had a more circumscribed and controversial component is equally important. His teachings and vision, for example, led to the establishment of the "Long House" religion that combines long-established Iroquois traditions with socioeconomic strategies that meshed with the needs of the times. As is often the case, furthermore, the innovative strivings of one generation are apt to become the conservative force of stability in the next. Indeed, the Long House tradition of today (the lengthened shadow of Handsome Lake's vision) tends to be embraced by the more traditional or orthodox element of Iroquois society. Thus, in the contemporary world, Handsome Lake's Long House religion represents a specific set of circumscribed principles embraced by the socially conservative Iroquois, while the more "liberal" or "progressive" segments of Iroquois society are often at odds with those who hold such beliefs.

Here, of course, I have no interest in entering into any debate regarding the pros and cons of the contemporary Long House religion and its vision for the future of Iroquois society. Ultimately, the Long House religion has been established for almost 200 years and it has evolved on its own since the death of Handsome Lake. My goal is merely to emphasize that in the early nineteenth century Handsome Lake recognized that his culture was under profound attack. Faced with these attacks, he forged a way to preserve his traditions, on the one hand, while adjusting them to prevailing circumstances on the other. Handsome Lake, furthermore, clearly saw a link between a healthy society and personal sobriety. Faced with rampant alcoholism among his people, he called for tight restrictions on alcohol and he was personally able to live a model life of recovery. Largely through his efforts, the Iroquois people reversed their downward plunge and reaffirmed their place as a proud Native nation.

Notes

1. The author's *The Path of Handsome Lake: A Model of Recovery for Native People* (Walle, 2004) provides an expanded view of these ideas and is recommended.

2. As a nation, the Iroquois did not have a pro-British policy; instead individual groups were allowed to make their own decision regarding the war. Most, however, sided with the British.

3. Others include promiscuous sexual behavior and the practice of witchcraft that was also disruptive to society and (according to Iroquois beliefs) injurious to specific people.

4. Handsome Lake was born in Avon, New York and promoted his antidrinking position in the early nineteenth century. He died in 1815 and the Long House religion, which is based on his teachings, began to flower in its present form around 1830. The Mormon religion first became an organized force in the 1830s (Joseph Smith, founder of the religion, reports he had a vision from God around 1820 and that in 1827 an angel helped him locate some manuscripts that became sacred Mormon texts. The religion was formally established in April 1830). This preliminary work of Joseph Smith in establishing the Mormon religion took place in and around Palmyra, New York, within easy reach of Handsome Lake's birthplace.

5. Important primary sources include A. F. C. Wallace's (1952) "Halliday Jackson's Journal to the Seneca Indians"; Thomas S. Abler's (1989) *Chainbreaker: The Revolutionary War Memoirs of Govern Blacksnake*, and

Arthur C. Parker's (1913) *The Code of Handsome Lake*. The most extensive (and respected) secondary work is A. F. C. Wallace's (1970) *The Death and Rebirth of the Seneca*. William Fenton and Elisabeth Tooker's (1951) "On the Development of the Handsome Lake Religion" is also insightful. It should be noted that there is an extensive research tradition on Handsome Lake and this is only a suggestive sampling. For those in the counseling profession, however, it is probably adequate.

References

Christopher, J. (1992) *How to stay sober: Recovery without religion*. Buffalo, New York: Promethus.

Christopher, J. (1997). Secular organizations for sobriety. In J. H. Lowinson, R. B. Ruiz, R. B. Milman, & J. G. Langrod (Eds.), *Substance abuse: A comprehensive textbook*. Baltimore: Williams and Williams.

Cloward, R. A., & Ohlin, L. E. (1960). *Delinquency and opportunity: A theory of delinquent gangs*. Glencoe, IL: Free Press.

Dodes, L. (2002). *The heart of addiction: A new approach for understanding and managing alcoholism and other addictive behaviors*. New York: Harper Collins.

Dressler, D. (1969). *Sociology: The study of human interaction*. New York: Alfred A. Knopf.

Erikson, K. T. (1966). *Wayward puritans: A study in the sociology of deviance*. New York: Wiley.

Fenton, W., & Tooker, E. (1951). On the development of the Handsome Lake religion. In W. N. Fenton (Ed.), *Symposium on local diversity in Iroquois culture*. Washington, DC: Bureau of American Ethnology.

Hovarth, A. T. (1997). Alternative support groups. In J. H. Lowinson, P. Ruiz, R. B. Millman, & J. G. Langrod (Eds.), *Substance abuse: A comprehensive textbook* (pp. 390-396). Baltimore: Williams and Wilkins.

Jankowski, M. S. (1991). *Islands in the street: Gangs and American urban society*. Berkeley: University of California Press.

Jenkins, P. (1992). *Intimate enemies: Moral panics in contemporary Great Britain*. New York: Aldine de Gruyter.

Kirkpatrick, J. (1978). *Turnabout: Help for a new life*. New York: Doubleday.

Kirkpatrick, J. (1990). *Stages of the new life program*. Quakertown, PA: Women for Sobriety.

MacIver, R. M. (1950). *The ramparts we guard*. New York: Macmillan.

Merton, R. (1957). *Social theory and social structure*. New York: The Free Press.

Napoleon, H. (1996). *Yunaraq: The way of being human*. Fairbanks: Alaska Native Knowledge Network.

Parker, A. C. (1913). *The code of Handsome Lake*. New York: State Education Department.

Peele, S. (1992). *Truth about addiction and recovery*. New York: Simon & Schuster.

Salzman, M. (2001). Cultural trauma and recovery: Perspectives from terror management theory. *Trauma, Violence and Abuse, 2*(2), 172-191.

Trimpey, J. (1989). *Rational recovery from alcoholism: The small book*. New York: Delacorte.

Wallace, A. F. C. (1952). Halliday Jackson's Journal to the Seneca Indians. *Pennsylvania History, 19*, 117-147, 325-349.

Wallace, A. F. C. (1970). *The death and rebirth of the Seneca*. New York: Knopf.

Walle, A. H. (1998). *Cultural tourism: A strategic focus*. Boulder CO: Westview Press.

Walle, A. H. (2004). *The path of Handsome Lake: A model of recovery for Native people*. Greenwich, CT: Information Age.

Chapter 3

Strategies of Intervention

INTRODUCTION

While much of what I have already presented is useful, it lacks specific guidelines regarding how to deal with clients who seek relief from their alcoholic behavior. The purpose of this chapter it to put some practitioner "meat" on the theoretic "bones" we have previously considered.

Below you will find a series of useful suggestions that can help you more effectively deal with clients. As you adjust the Handsome Lake program to your unique professional style, some of these ideas may be useful.

As I have repeatedly emphasized, Native people who experience problems with substance abuse often need to come to grips with their cultural heritage and their relationship to it. The suggestions in this book provide tools that can help Native clients do so in a structured and meaningful manner. In recent years, providing appropriate therapy to diverse people has become a high profile activity and the Handsome Lake program provides a practical tool for helping Native people. It is a flexible method that can be used either as a primary tool of therapy or as a supplemental program. Each option is discussed.

A PRIMARY PROGRAM

Interventions that serve Native substance abusers can employ the Handsome Lake program as a primary vehicle of therapy. Although many Native people may be largely unaware of or alienated from their heritage, cultural issues can still trigger their alcoholic

drinking. As a result, the Handsome Lake program can be of significant value to a wide range of people.

As mentioned above, many other programs of recovery do not overtly deal with cultural issues and their relationship to dysfunction. As a result, they do little to help Native people cope with the fact that their cultures may be under severe attack and/or that some Native substance abusers may be alienated from their traditions.

The Twelve Steps program and many other strategies of recovery, for example, seldom deal with the stress caused by the weakening of cultural traditions. These programs tend to covertly assume that a healthy and robust cultural foundation exists to which recovering clients can return once they begin to get their life in order.

Native people, however, often need to cope with the fact that their cultures are under severe attack. In addition, they may be alienated from their heritage. The Handsome Lake Program is specifically designed to deal with such issues. As a result, it is often especially appropriate therapy for Native clients.

STRUCTURING THE PROGRAM, SETTING THE STAGE

Specific Native clients may or may not be aware that cultural decline and/or a disconnection from their heritage might be triggering their substance abuse. If you suspect this is the case, a good first step is to make clients aware of how a weakened cultural heritage and/or personal alienation from it can be hurtful.

Some clients will readily recognize this impact; others will not. As a result, encouraging general discussions regarding the importance of cultures and traditions may be a useful opening gambit before delving into more specific discussions.

One way of doing so is for the therapist to recommend (or discuss) Harold Napoleon's analysis of cultural decline among the Yup'ik of Alaska as analyzed in his *Yuuyaraq: The Way of Being Human* (1996).[1] This book has the advantages of being short and being presented in laymen's terms. Napoleon's experiences, furthermore, largely parallel those of Handsome Lake.

When presenting the example of Handsome Lake, it is good to start by observing that he seemed to be an incurable alcoholic, but recovered and became an influential leader who helped his people. By focusing on Handsome Lake's personal example of recovery, clients can be encouraged to believe that they, too, can succeed in their quest of sobriety.

If the therapist introduces Handsome Lake, as a Native alcoholic who successfully recovered, therapy based on his legacy can be presented as a credible opportunity. The way in which Handsome Lake combined personal recovery with cultural renewal and the embrace of his Native culture needs to be emphasized. This introduction can lead to a discussion of the Path of Handsome Lake and the Landmarks of the Path.

In general, clients need to be encouraged to view themselves as Native people who may have been injured and traumatized by an environment where their heritage was ignored and devalued. They might have been active participants in this disrespect, although this will not always be the case.

It might also be beneficial for clients to be reminded that people are not always conscious of the impact of a Native identity and how it influences their behavior. As a result, clients may need to think about who they really are. A greater awareness may be built by having clients complete outside assignments (preferably written) in which they consider these issues on their own so they can come to therapy sessions ready to discuss what they have learned after a period of independent self-reflection.[2]

Many Native cultures, furthermore, have complied and published lists of their values.[3] If such a list exists for your client's Native culture, it can be used as a point of departure. If not, various lists that are readily available might serve in a stopgap capacity. If a vibrant and robust Native community exists locally, the therapist may have access to important elders and other carriers of Native traditions. In any case, the idea is to combine recovery with a greater cultural awareness. The Handsome Lake program is distinctive in that it provides a systematic way to do so.

The reader should also remember that many people are aware of the importance of their Native culture and a number of therapy programs that are based on Native traditions. Typically, these programs help people connect with their traditions and use them as tools of recovery. Many programs work to accomplish these goals and this book recognizes and applauds all these efforts. My goal is to provide a programmatic means of doing so.

Therapy often needs to be structured in ways that draw attention toward the Native cultural heritage. Showcasing the conflicts between the Native and mainstream cultures can be an important tool. Clients need to consider what has been lost as Native cultures have been weakened and/or as individuals have become alienated from their traditions.

PRIMARY INDIVIDUAL COUNSELING

Individual counseling, by nature, is a "one-on-one" activity involving a therapist and counselor working together, largely in isolation. Although some group sessions may occur, individual therapy is largely self-contained. This arrangement possesses both strengths and weaknesses. Although individual counseling is closely attuned to the needs of a particular client, it does not benefit from the power of synergism (an important strength of much group therapy.) A major benefit in individual counseling, however, is that the client is protected from possible shame and humiliation that could result from dealing with sensitive issues within a group context.

While in group therapy newcomers may be able to "pick up" the essentials of the program by watching and listening to veteran participants and by being informally coached by them, in individual therapy clients and counselors may be required to exert, considerable time and effort discussing the basics of the program. Getting over the hurdle of these preliminaries can make progress painfully slow at first. A useful alternative is for the client to simultaneously be involved in some kind of group counseling or self-help activities that are centered on the Handsome Lake program. These activities can serve as a supplement to "one on one" therapy sessions and provide a grounding in the program.

A short description of the Handsome Lake method written for clients (*Recovery the Native Way*) is available from Information Age, the publisher of this book; it can be a useful tool in this regard. A consumable workbook that helps clients work through various issues suggested by the Handsome Lake program is also available from Information Age. By using these tools, individual therapy sessions can avoid dwelling on basic information and, as a result, more time can be spent discussing the client's specific circumstances and needs.

In any event, clients should be consciously aware of the Path of Handsome Lake and the Landmarks of the Path and they should be given copies of both. Posters of each are provided in an appendix of this book. The posters are also available in *Recovery the Native Way*, the clients' book. Having the posters available can help clients to focus on cultural issues and how they relate to both alcoholism and recovery.

On many occasions, a particular client may have been previously involved in therapy and counseling and have prior experience with various methods of treatment. These clients may harbor preconceptions regarding what to expect in therapy and/or conclude that the program will probably not help them. If so, the differences between the Handsome Lake program and other programs of therapy need to be emphasized. A good initial strategy may be to ask the client about earlier therapy, what methods were used, and the client's opinion of the experience with them. These questions can open up the conversation in useful and revealing ways.

As has been emphasized throughout this book, the Handsome Lake method is primarily concerned with the individuals' cultural heritage and its impact on substance abuse and recovery. Realizing that recovery is often linked to a strong and vibrant cultural heritage, the Handsome Lake method emphasizes that people often benefit from connecting with their cul-

tural heritage in intimate ways. This process of cultural renewal overlays, while not crowding out, the personal work that is required for a healthy and lasting recovery.

As argued above, the cultural heritage, when functioning properly, can serve as a profound source of comfort and strength for people. It can also serve as a buffer against stress and anxiety. In these ways, a person's heritage can provide a powerful means of mitigating tensions that otherwise could trigger substance abuse. By strengthening the Native culture and by helping individuals to relate to their heritage in positive ways, the stress and anxiety that spawns dysfunctional behavior can be reduced.

Individual therapy can effectively explore how and why particular people began their substance abuse. In such a one-on-one setting, the client can deal with personal issues and do so in a private context (discussed further in Table 3.1). Thus, individual, one-on-one therapy can be a useful means of applying the Handsome Lake program. For various reasons, however, group therapy may emerge as the most appropriate or practical vehicle of therapy. It is discussed below.

PRIMARY GROUP THERAPY

As indicated above, individual "one on one" counseling has the advantage of focusing upon the needs of a specific client, but it inevitably takes place in relative isolation. Group therapy, in contrast, is a collective activity. Indeed, therapy groups often develop an identity and camaraderie that have significant collective value. The interpersonal dynamics that result from group therapy is often powerful and effective. This book does not have a preference for either type of therapy, but it does emphasize that individual and group therapies both have distinctive roles, strengths, and weaknesses. And, as indicated above, group and individual therapy can often work in tandem with each another in positive ways that resonate from each other.

Some therapy groups are ongoing, although specific group members may come and go over time. Where this is true, knowledge of the Handsome Lake program will emerge and become a permanent feature of that group. As indicated above, where the group is permanent and ongoing, existing members can orient

Table 3.1.   Primary/Individual Therapy

	Overview	*Analysis*
Relationship	A strong counselor/client relationship exists that seeks to explore the cultural heritage of the client in order to combat tendencies toward substance abuse.	In individual therapy, the counselor and the client are able to focus upon issues that concern the individual and the Native culture. The cloistered nature of the relationship prevents public shaming and humiliation.
Worldview	The fact that significant cultural stress can trigger individual dysfunction is emphasized. Building cultural awareness and developing a comfort with the Native heritage can be therapeutic.	The Handsome Lake program is different from mainstream programs of recovery because it deals with the Native culture as typically under stress. Acknowledging this situation, the program centers on individual vulnerability that is triggered by assaults on culture and/or the client's alienation from his/her heritage and traditions.
Expectation	Working as a team, the client and counselor expect to explore the cultural traditions of the client in order to overcome triggers that can lead to dysfunction.	The counselor and client expect to explore aspects of the cultural and heritage in ways that enhance the ability to combat dysfunction. There is an expectation that recovery can result from greater cultural awareness.
Intervention	The Path of Handsome Lake and the Landmarks of the Path are employed to help people get in touch with their heritage and, thereby, become less vulnerable to dysfunction resulting from anxiety related to cultural stress.	The intervention consists of practicing the Path of Handsome Lake and the Landmarks of the Path. These interventions build confidence in the ability to achieve sobriety while introducing the elements of the cultural heritage that are useful in recovery.
Discussion	The client and the counselor are involved in a program of therapy that is primarily based on the Path of Handsome Lake/Landmarks of the Path. Other methods (such as the Twelve Steps program) may be discussed in order to more effectively explore the Handsome Lake method and its benefits. The focus is on the client's Native culture and the client's relationship to it.	

Note: The issues dealt with in this table (relationhip, worldview, expectation, intervention) derive from Fischer, Jobe, and Atkinson (1988). The influence of that model on my work is more fully discuss in my book *The Path of Handsome Lake: A Model of Recovery for Native People* (2004),

newcomers and make them aware of the basics of the program. This can save the therapist time and effort. Some ad hoc groups, in contrast, may have been created for a special purpose, have a limited life, and cease to exist at a scheduled time. When a new group begins (be it a temporary, ad hoc group or the beginning of on ongoing group activity), the facilitator will need to outline the basics of the Handsome Lake program and how it differs from other strategies of recovery. As already mentioned, the tools provided by Information Age Publishing are useful in this regard.

In specific, everyone in the group needs to clearly understand how the Handsome Lake program works, why it is structured in the way it is, and what it seeks to accomplish. As emphasized above, cultural stress and/or decline coupled with the possible alienation of individuals from their heritage can trigger dysfunctional behavior. In contrast, by rebuilding the strength of the culture and the clients' relationship to it, in contrast, tools of recovery can be developed.

A part of this process may involve a positive introduction (or reintroduction) of the Native culture to participants in the group. A particular therapy group, however, will probably be composed of members of various Native cultures; as a result, the group cannot merely focus on a specific set of traditions that are linked to one homogeneous group or a unique Native culture.[4] Instead, the program needs to help all members of the group to recognize the power and value of their particular cultural heritage. By doing so, each member can better understand how cultural decline and personal alienation from a cultural heritage might trigger alcoholism. See Table 3.2.

While in some circumstances, the Handsome Lake program may dominate, on other occasions, it will be used in conjunction with other methods of therapy. Is inevitable that better established programs of recovery will often dominate. As a result, dealing with situations where the Handsome Lake program shares the stage (and often serves in a subordinate role) needs to be discussed.

A SUPPLEMENTAL PROGRAM

In reality, of course, other methods of recovery tend to dominate alcoholism treatment programs. The most prevalent method is the Twelve Steps program developed by Alcoholics Anonymous. As discussed, these programs tend to ignore the issue of cultural stress. The Twelve Steps program, for example, does not focus on factors related to the decline of Native cultures nor does it seek to address the alienation that many Native people feel toward their traditions. Although the Twelve Steps program is not antagonistic to the Handsome Lake method (and other culturally centered therapies), it tends to turn a blind eye to hurtful pressures and challenges that face many Native people. Due to this gap, the Handsome Lake program can serve a valuable supplemental service for Native people seeking recovery.

While not conflicting with other strategies of recovery, such as the Twelve Steps program, the Handsome

Table 3.2.   Primary Group Therapy

	Overview	Analysis
Relationship	A group of people, monitored and led by a facilitator provides a forum where people can explore their cultural heritages in order to combat tendencies toward substance abuse.	In group therapy, the facilitator focuses the group's attention around issues concerned with Native cultures. The nature of the group facilitates a free-wheeling approach that can provide a richer and more varied therapy.
Worldview	Discussions emphasize how cultural stress can trigger dysfunction. Strengthening the cultural heritage and building the group's cultural awareness can be therapeutic to the group, in general, and to individuals, in specific.	The Handsome Lake method is different from other programs of recovery because it deals with the stress that Native cultures often experience. The program centers on how group members may be vulnerable to assaults on the culture and personal alienation from their cultural heritage.
Expectation	Working in a group setting, members expect to explore each other's cultural traditions in order to overcome vulnerabilities that can lead to dysfunction. Respectful confrontation and criticism are often positive activities.	The facilitator and the group expect to explore aspects of the cultures and heritages of the members in ways that help all to overcome dysfunction. There is an expectation that recovery can result from greater cultural awareness and becoming comfortable with one's traditions.
Intervention	The group employs the Path of Handsome Lake and the Landmarks of the Path so each person can get more in touch with their heritage and become less vulnerable to dysfunction resulting from anxiety related to cultural stress and/or alienation from a cultural heritage.	In group therapy, the Path of Handsome Lake and the Landmarks of the Path are practiced in order to provide insights to both personal and group problems. These interventions build confidence in the ability to achieve sobriety by strengthening the culture and the individual's relationship to it.
Discussion	The group and its facilitator are involved in a program of therapy that is primarily based on the Handsome Lake method. Although other methods (such as the Twelve Steps program) may be discussed, the are subordinate to the Handsome Lake method and its focus on the clients' cultural heritage and its impacts.	

Lake method can draw attention toward the cultural heritage of clients in useful and therapeutic ways.

The Twelve Steps program, for example, does not deal with the fact that a cultural heritage may be weakened and that this situation can trigger dysfunction. Because of the structure and orientation of mainstream programs, the health of the culture is not addressed as a significant issue. Many Native peoples, however, suffer because the culture has been significantly undermined and/or because they have become distanced from it. The Handsome Lake program is a useful supplement of treatment that fills in the gaps left by mainstream programs.

When the Handsome Lake program is used in conjunction with some other program of recovery, clients need to be kept conscious of (1) the similarities and (2) the differences in each program and how each can usefully supplement the other. The lack of conflict between these programs needs to be emphasized. Each program should be dealt with as an equally valid (but different) component of recovery.

A good way to introduce this point might be to observe that people can simultaneously be a part of their traditional Native culture and the mainstream world. Discussions can seek to establish areas where clients feel they are members of the mainstream world and, in contrast, where they believe they are strongly influenced by their heritage and traditions. It is important to emphasize that these two worlds may be in significant conflict and the resulting tensions can trigger tensions, stress, anxiety, and dysfunction.

INDIVIDUAL SUPPLEMENTAL COUNSELING

Individual supplemental counseling has the same strengths and weaknesses as primary individual counseling (see discussion above). While centered around the needs of a particular person, it does not benefit from group synergism.

In individual supplemental counseling, it is vital to determine how the needs of the client can be addressed by conventional therapy in tandem with more culturally sensitive strategies, such as the Handsome Lake method. As indicated above, mainstream programs (such as the Twelve Steps program) are neither strongly attuned to cultural stress/cultural decline nor do they deal with the possibility that people have become alienated from their traditional culture. Probing the client to determine the role that each program lays can provide a way to better understand how therapy should proceed. If possible, written assignments prepared outside of the therapy session as "homework" can help the client think about these issues. Tools that have been developed and are available from Information Age Publishing may be useful in this regard.

The therapist needs to determine how the Handsome Lake program can best be applied and how it can be most effectively integrated with other programs of recovery. What benefits will the particular client receive? How can the benefits of different programs be positively blended with each other?

The Handsome Lake program should be presented as a specialized therapy that has the potential to provide some people with the cultural insights they need to recover. One useful strategy is to explain to the client that the Twelve Steps program is not equipped to deal cultural decline or with the pain that people feel when they are alienated from their heritage. Pointing out the strengths and limitations of each program, the client and counselor can discuss the degree to which each program should be incorporated in the therapeutic process.

Having done so, the program needs to be implemented with reference to the usual tactics of individual therapy. An overview of the program presented in Table 3.3.

When using the Handsome Lake program in a supplemental capacity, the array of options becomes more complex because no firm and predefined template exists on which to base therapy. Instead, the counselor needs to consider the particular needs of the client and how they can best be addressed. Although creating an appropriate mix of therapeutic tools can be difficult (and may be more of an art than a science), doing so allows the program to be tailored to the needs of particular people. Be careful; striking a proper balance can be difficult and programs should not be applied in routine ways.

Table 3.3.   Supplemental Individual Therapy

	Overview	*Analysis*
Relationship	A strong counselor/client relationship exists that seeks to employ the Handsome Lake method along with other tools of recovery in the most effective way. The client and counselor work together to devise the proper structure of their unique program.	In situations where other programs are being employed along with the Handsome Lake model, the client and counselor need to work to determine the appropriate role of each program. There is no universally "right" or "wrong" strategy because different clients have their own needs and vulnerabilities.
Worldview	The Handsome Lake method and conventional strategies of treatment each have their strengths and weaknesses. The counselor and client need to determine how each method will be worked into a program of recovery. The resulting decision can help determine the appropriate tactics to be employed.	Although the therapeutic relationship may employ a variety of methods, this does not mean that they are in conflict in any way. Instead, each method is able to serve the client in a specific manner. After determining the client's needs, the value and scope of each method can be determined and a strategy that best serves the client can be devised.
Expectation	Interacting as a dyad, the client and counselor will work toward recovery in an agreed-on manner. They expect results to reflect their collective orientations.	Because the expectations will, to a large extent, be a function of a shared worldview of the counselor and client, they will evolve a unique therapeutic relationship. Formally establishing a list of expectations and putting them in writing is a good strategy.
Intervention	An appropriate intervention will be based on the perspectives and expectations of the client and counselor. Components of both the Handsome Lake method and other therapies will be present. The final formula will reflect the needs of the client.	The intervention consists of practicing the Handsome Lake method and other programs of therapy in a way that suits the unique client. To whatever degree the client has been impacted by cultural decline and/or has been alienated from his/her heritage, the Handsome Lake model will be of vital importance. Nonetheless, there is no inherent conflict between different methods employed.
Discussion	The client and the counselor are involved in a program where the Handsome Lake model is used in a supplemental fashion. In such situations, the role of different strategies of recovery needs to be determined. Both the client and counselor need to be aware that the Handsome Lake model and other strategies of recovery are not in conflict, but are merely different tools to be used as required. Since each client will typically have a unique set of needs and expectations, it is a good idea to create a written list of expectations and a formal menu of how various methods will be implemented.	

SUPPLEMENTAL GROUP THERAPY

In group therapy, as indicated earlier, the group has an existence that transcends the individual. This characteristic has both advantages and disadvantages.

In a supplemental capacity, the Path of Handsome Lake is used in conjunction with some other method such as the Twelve Steps program. As we saw above, however, conventional programs typically do not forcefully deal with cultural stress and alienation. We also saw that in many cases the members of the group will come from various backgrounds and cultures. Situations where all group members are from exactly the same culture will be an exception to the rule.

It is a good idea to have all the group members share various aspects of their cultural heritage and the pressures and stresses that their culture faces. This can lead to discussions of anxieties that are triggered by cultural stress and the trauma that exist when people are alienated from their heritage. When specific examples of cultural stress, conflict, and anxiety are analyzed, they can be discussed in general terms so all group members can relate to them. Nevertheless, the specifics issues and challenges faced by individual clients need to be recognized and acknowledged.

It is important to emphasize that the Handsome Lake method is not in conflict or in competition with any other strategy of recovery. See Table 3.4.

Thus, on many occasions, the Handsome Lake method will be used in a supplemental manner. Since there is no inherent conflict between the Handsome Lake program and other strategies of therapy, it can be employed in a wide number of ways.

CONCLUSION

According to Fischer, Jobe, and Atkinson (1998), multicultural therapy consists of at least the following components: (1) a therapeutic relationship exists, (2) those

Table 3.4.   Supplemental Group Therapy

	Overview	*Analysis*
Relationship	The group seeks to explore the advantages of the Handsome Lake program and other methods of recovery. The group and facilitator understand that different clients have their own needs and that each member will practice a unique program of recovery.	Where other programs are being employed along with the Handsome Lake model, the group should acknowledge that different members have their own unique needs. Members must respect the programs of recovery practiced by others and understand that there is no inherently "right" strategy, because different members have their own unique goals and issues.
Worldview	Both the Handsome Lake method and conventional strategies of treatment have their strengths and weaknesses. The group and the facilitator need to underscore that each program is valuable, but that different people will need to implement these tools in their own ways.	Although the therapeutic relationship may employ two different methods or strategies, this does not mean that they are in conflict in any way. Instead, each program may serve various group members in a helpful manner. By allowing all group members to structure their own strategy of recovery, each will benefit from both self-determinism and the benefits of group solidarity.
Expectation	The group and facilitator will work toward recovery in the manner agreed on by the group. Nonetheless, the structure will allow for individual differences. All within the group will be respectful of differences.	Because various strategies are combined, the shared perspective of the group will acknowledge individual variations. As a result, the expectations of each member will be unique. Formally establishing a list of expectations is a good strategy.
Intervention	An appropriate intervention will be based on the perspectives and expectations of the group and the needs of individual members. Components of both the Handsome Lake method and conventional therapy will fit into the final formula chosen by individual members.	The intervention consists of practicing the Handsome Lake and conventional methods in a way that conforms to the group consensus and meets the needs of individuals. To whatever degree the group members have been impacted by cultural decline and/or by alienation from their heritage, the Handsome Lake method is useful. Nonetheless, there is no inherent conflict between the Handsome Lake method and other programs of recovery.
Discussion	The group and the facilitator are involved in a program where the Handsome Lake method is used in a supplemental fashion as needed to serve the group and its individual clients. It is vital to emphasize that the Handsome Lake method and other strategies of recovery are not in conflict, but are merely different tools to be used as required. Since each member will typically have a unique set of needs and expectations, it is a good idea for each member to create a written list of expectations and perceived needs.	

involved in this relationship have some kind of a shared worldview, (3) The person receiving help has certain expectations, and (4) some kind of ritual or intervention occurs. In this chapter, the Handsome Lake program was analyzed according to these criteria. So viewed, it clearly met the criteria of therapy as presented by Fischer et al.

While the Handsome Lake program provides a specific method of therapy, it can be used in a variety of ways. On some occasions, it may emerge as the primary vehicle of therapy while, on other occasions, it may serve a supplemental role. As a result, the Handsome Lake program can be applied in four distinct ways, (1) individual primary therapy, (2) individual supplemental therapy, (3) group primary therapy, and (4) group supplemental therapy. By providing guidelines for each use, the flexibility of the program is demonstrated.

NOTES

1.   Those seeking copies of Napoleon's book can acquire them by contacting the Alaska Native Knowledge Network University of Alaska at Fairbanks, Fairbanks, Alaska 99775. The price is reasonable.

2.   The Alaska Native Knowledge Network, University of Alaska at Fairbanks, Fairbanks, Alaska 99775.

3.   Again the Alaska Native Knowledge Network can provide these tools at nominal cost.

4.   Even among members of the same Native culture there are often many groups that are unique in their own distinctive ways. Among the Athabascan people of Alaska, for example, the culture is made up of many subgroups, each having its own traditions and distinctictions. As a result, finding a group of Native people who are "identical" is almost impossible.

REFERENCES

Fischer, A. R., Jobe, L. M., & Atkinson, D. R. (1998). Reconceptualizing multicultural counseling: Universal healing conditions in a culturally specific context. *The Counseling Psychologist, 26*(4), 525-588.

Napoleon, H. (1996). *Yuuyaraq: The way of being human.* Fairbanks: Alaska Native Knowledge Network.

Chapter 4

Suggestions for Therapy

INTRODUCTION

Being newly developed, no lore and grassroots suggestions have grown up around the Handsome Lake program of recovery. As a result, those who want to apply this tool of recovery may experience difficulty because they will have access to little practical advice. Anticipating this problem, the present chapter provides an array of "hands on" tactics that can help you begin to employ the program.

We will first discuss how to apply the Handsome Lake program, what it can accomplish, and how it can help Native people recover from substance abuse. After these discussions have been provided, specific suggestions will be offered. A number of ideas regarding "specialty" meetings/sessions and how they can be conducted are also discussed. Hopefully, these tips will help therapists devise ways to apply the Handsome Lake method in an organized and productive manner.

GENERAL OBSERVATIONS

As discussed throughout this book, many Native cultures are under stress and this situation often creates anxieties that can trigger dysfunctional behavior, such as substance abuse. By building a positive and productive relationship with the person's culture and heritage, anxiety and the dysfunction that accompanies it can be reduced. As emphasized earlier, the Twelve Steps program does not actively focus upon the stress to which cultures, especially Native cultures, are subjected. As a result of this limitation, the Twelve Steps program is not well equipped to deal with issues that are related to the individual's cultural heritage and the fact that when traditions and heritages are under attack, substance abuse easily result.

The Handsome Lake method provides a useful alternative that deals with these vital cultural issues. Handsome Lake, as you have learned, was an historic Native leader who recognized the need to strengthen the culture; he suggested a program that simultaneously restores the culture to health, on the one hand, while helping individual people to overcome their substance abuse, on the other. Even though Handsome Lake lived in the eighteenth and nineteenth centuries, his work clearly reflects the findings of modern social scientists and psychologists as well as the insights of contemporary Native leaders (such as Harold Napoleon) who also seek to overcome substance abuse by embracing their cultural identity. Given the validity, usefulness, and timeliness of Handsome Lake's wisdom, this book suggests a program of therapy that is based on his culturally oriented principles.

MEETINGS: AN OVERVIEW

Therapeutic meetings possess the advantages of (1) more efficiently serving several individuals simultaneously (2) coupled with the power of group dynamics. Meetings provide a popular and proven method of both self-help and professionally managed therapy. The group method has proven itself within a variety of contexts and it has been usefully applied within both mainstream and Native cultural contexts. Examples will be discussed below.

THE TWELVE STEPS PROGRAM AND ITS LEGACY

The methods associated with Twelve Steps program are classic and widely known tools of recovery. Most basically, this method started out as a self-help activity in which people collectively sought to overcome their common struggle with substance abuse. The Twelve Steps program largely relies on the benefits that can be derived from participation within a group context. The Twelve Steps program is designed to (1) provide the support of a group that encourages participants to find counsel and comfort as they (2) work together to overcome their common problem. From the earliest days of the Alcoholics Anonymous, the Twelve Steps program has been used to help substance abusers to band together for their common benefit and, in the process, gain a collective strength that, individually, they lack.

Many substance abusers seeking recovery, furthermore, have some prior experience with Alcoholics Anonymous/Narcotics Anonymous and the Twelve Steps program and, therefore, they are familiar with the method's group dynamics and the structure of meetings As a result, other therapeutic organizations and strategies of recovery can easily build on this strategy of treatment.

THE TALKING CIRCLE LEGACY

While the Twelve Steps program was suggested by the experiences of Bill Wilson and Dr. Bob in the 1930s and later refined and codified by Alcoholics Anonymous, Native peoples possess their own in powerful and therapeutic techniques of group intervention. One such tradition is commonly known at the "Talking Circle." Basically, a talking circle is a group of people who meet in a largely unstructured and democratic forum. Those participating within a talking circle context agree that the person who currently "has the floor" has the freedom to discuss anything that he or she deems important; they are allowed to do so without censure or interference from others. Typically, the speaker holds some object from nature (such as a feather) that grants the right to speak. After a person has finished talking, the object (and the

forum) is passed to the next person who can either speak or pass it along in silence. While holding the object, a person has the freedom to say anything on whatever topic without interference, censure, and without the threat of retaliation once the meeting is over. In addition, what is said within the context of a talking circle is viewed as confidential and people are forbidden to repeat or discuss what was said once the talking circle ends. Thus, the talking circle provides an open forum that facilitates dealing with troubling issues that cannot be comfortably or appropriately addressed within other contexts.

This kind of communication has proved to be very useful in many circumstances and it is a commonly used technique among many Native American peoples. In addition, various therapists and self-help advocates have developed strategies for using the talking circle concept within the context of substance abuse therapy to assist Native substance abusers seeking recovery.

DISCUSSION

The Twelve Steps program and the talking circle both allow participants to speak their mind without fear, censure, or interference; thus in Twelve Steps meetings "cross talk" (responding directly to someone's comments, especially in confrontational ways) is forbidden. And in both Twelve Steps meetings and talking circles, what is discussed is expected to remain confidential and not discussed outside the group. Thus, significant parallels exist between the mainstream Twelve Steps program and the talking circle traditions of Native people.

SPECIFIC TYPES OF MEETINGS

Group therapy has long been practiced within substance abuse therapy. Group meetings have an important role in both self-help activities and in professionally managed therapy. Each option is discussed.

SELF-HELP MEETINGS

Alcoholics Anonymous and Narcotics Anonymous, of course, are self-help organizations that are independent of any formal structure, even though they employ the Twelve Steps program. Emphasizing self-help, Alcoholics Anonymous and Narcotics Anonymous provide a meeting format that is run by lay people who seek personal recovery. As a result, they resemble a democratic, open forum. In reality, however, many meetings are clearly influenced by particular people who somehow gain and exert power on it. In addition, some strong willed people seek to forcefully impact all they touch, including self-help meetings.

Many recovering substance abusers prefer self-help meetings to professionally provided therapy because they believe (and sometimes vocally assert) that professional therapists are only "in it for the money." Other participants may point to the fact that those who participate in self-help groups are "real drunks" like themselves and, therefore, self-help meetings provide true insights that are not diluted by over-intellectual mumbo jumbo. Self-help organizations are run by lay people and they lack a formal leadership; these characteristics give their meetings both strengths and weaknesses. Since self-help meetings are not facilitated by a professional, they may "get off the track" and/or some questionable ideas may be championed without being adequately challenged. Nonetheless, these meetings are free to the public, populated by well meaning individuals who possess experience in fighting substance abuse, and most attendees take what is said with a grain of salt. Indeed, one of the classic and often repeated slogans within Twelve Steps meetings is "take what you need and leave the rest."

By the same token, self-help meetings that revolve around the Handsome Lake model may possess these same potential strengths and weaknesses. Learning from earlier examples of self-help, those who seek to establish Handsome Lake self-help meetings need to consider these issues in order to create the most effective forum.

FACILITATOR MANAGED MEETINGS

While Alcoholics Anonymous and Narcotics Anonymous are self-help groups consisting of lay people, the ambience of these programs and many of their techniques have been adapted for use within a professional therapeutic context. Under such circumstances, a professional facilitator, therapist, or counselor manages meetings within the context of treatment. These meetings, by their very nature, tend to be more structured than self-help meetings. Although the facilitator may allow and encourage a degree of flexibility, meetings are usually orchestrated or directed by the leader in some kind of overt or covert manner. In these meetings, there is a greater chance that the topic being discussed will be chosen by the facilitator. In such settings, facilitators have a degree of authority that can be used if clients get off the topic, are offensive, drag on too long, and so forth. And while self-help meetings are purely voluntary (even if some attendees may be court mandated), attendance in facilitator-managed meetings tends to be scheduled and obligatory.

While the cultural focus of the Handsome Lake program makes it unique, many of the tactics and structures developed for Twelve Steps therapy meetings can be adapted and adjusted for use within the Handsome Lake program. Since many participants in the Handsome Lake program will probably be familiar with the Twelve Steps format, these veterans of therapy and self-help can more easily adjust to the new program.

SPECIALITY MEETINGS AND THEIR PURPOSES

Both within self-help programs and a professionally managed regimen of therapy, certain types of meetings have a particular purpose or ambience. Some meetings occur on a regular schedule, but the topic or tone of the meeting is not preordained and a leader or some other participant will suggest a topic. Other meetings, in contrast, have a structure, purpose, or topic that is a regular and ongoing feature of that group. Pressing circumstances, furthermore, may dictate adopting a special format for a specific meeting. Varieties of meetings that fit well with within the Handsome Lake method of recovery include:

AN INTRODUCTION TO THE PROGRAM

The Handsome Lake method is new and it will need to be introduced to clients. In order to facilitate this process, a 12-session introduction to the method can be used. It is discussed, complete with a detailed treatment plan, in chapter 8 of this book. This 12-session program makes use of the description of the program written for clients (*Recovery the Native Way*) and the consumable workbook that accompanies it. Both of these tools are available from Information Age Publishing.

Path Meetings

A common feature of Alcoholics Anonymous is that various meetings are known to be "Twelve Steps" and "Twelve Traditions" meetings. Thus, those meetings typically deal with one of the Twelve Steps or the Twelve Traditions that underlie the Twelve Steps program. Typically, these meetings are held at a particular time (possibly on a special night once a week). This method provides a recurring reinforcement of the key principles of the program, and it has proven to be useful, constructive and enjoyable for many members. Newcomers, furthermore are often attracted to (or directed to) these meetings because they provide an ongoing overview of the program.

Borrowing from the proven strategies of Alcoholics Anonymous, a Path Meeting can provide a way of focusing on key elements of the Handsome Lake method. The meeting deals with a specific step in the path and continues in an endless cycle. By doing so, the main issues in the program are discussed on a regular schedule. Doing so provides an introduction to the program for newcomers while reinforcing the essence of the program to ongoing members. As with AA Step meetings, Path Meetings can be useful in helping individuals to internalize the program. Such a format can be useful for that reason. Various techniques for managing and structuring a Path meeting can be devised. A meeting may begin with some sort of reading followed by discussions that are based on it. Or, perhaps, the meeting might focus on a particular aspect of the particular step under discussion. Perhaps a talking circle format will be chosen in order to discuss a particular part of the Path, etc. Typically, a particular meeting will adopt an ongoing format so participants will know what to expect.

Landmark Meetings

Just as Path meetings can reinforce the essence of the program, Landmark meetings can remind participants of strategies and tactics that can be employed when working the program. As with path meetings, Landmark meetings can be scheduled at a special time and they can discuss the Landmarks in some type of rotating order. And like Path meetings, Landmark meetings can help new members learn the essence of the program while serving as a useful reminder to veterans.

Qualifying Meetings

One popular category of meeting from Alcoholics Anonymous and Narcotics Anonymous is generally known as a "qualifying meeting." These meetings feature a guest speaker (or a group member) who provides a discussion regarding why he/she is "qualifies" to be a member of the group. In general, this involves some kind of description of problems caused by drinking/drugging and how the qualifier has been able to forge a long-term path toward sobriety (or, perhaps, why this has not occurred.) Thus, the discussants provide proof that they are "qualified" to discuss substance abuse as an insider.

There is no reason why this kind of meeting cannot be a useful part of the Handsome Lake program, although it is good to encourage the speaker to focus on cultural themes.

Talking Circle Meetings

Although any meeting can embrace a talking circle format in an impromptu sort of way, some meetings may be designated as talking circle meetings and will always be structured in such a manner. Other meetings, not permanently structured around the talking circle concept, may embrace the format as circumstances dictate.

Talking circle meetings are particularly useful when certain issues need to be discussed in an open forum and/or when certain members tend to dominate to the point where the opinions and feelings of others could be overshadowed. The talking circle format can also emphasize the fact that the participants are Native people, by embracing the talking circle format. Because the talking circle format offers parity to all, it is especially helpful if certain shy or more reserved participants need the floor; this is especially true when controversy is involved.

Cultural Diversity Meetings

A key element of the Handsome Lake method is that a person's cultural heritage is valuable both in its own right and because it serves as a strong buffer against anxiety and adversity. At the same time, this background can create vulnerabilities that need to be addressed.

On many occasions, however, people have trouble understanding the heritage of others; as a result, confusions can arise when people lack the skills and knowledge that are needed to empathize with and provide support to each other. In view of the fact that many Native people suffer trauma due to assaults on their cultures, Native people seeking to recover from alcoholism often need the support and understanding of their fellows. The distinctiveness of particular cultures also needs to be recognized.

In addition, since many people have been exposed to generic modes of therapy that attempt to provide a general and universal program of treatment, Native people often need to be reminded of cultural diversity and how it can simultaneously provide strength and create vulnerabilities.

Special meetings can deal with and celebrate cultural diversity. By doing so, participants can learn to accept themselves (and others) for who they are and, as a result, they can better understand each other. Such an atmosphere can help relieve the anxiety that often result when people fail to acknowledge who they really are and/or when they are not treated in appropriate ways due to misunderstandings.

Achievement Meetings

One of the frequent types of meeting in Alcoholics Anonymous and Narcotics Anonymous involves celebrations of personal achievements. Many of these meetings mark a milestone in a participant's recovery, such as the anniversary of sobriety.

People who are recovering from substance abuse often have a past track record of failure and disappointment; they need to be reminded that goals can be achieved. Recognizing the achievements of others is one way to do so. As a result, achievement meetings are a meaningful addition to any program of recovery. Some groups may have regularly scheduled achievement meetings (on the first Monday of every month, for example.) And when an especially significant achievement occurs in the life of some participant, it is often possible to have an impromptu achievement meeting to celebrate the event. Many people in recovery affirm that achievement meetings help them to maintain their confidence and motivation. As a result, opportunities to celebrate personal achievements should be viewed as good therapy for those being recognized and an excellent example for the meeting as a whole.

Relapse Meetings

A sad reality of recovery is that many people backslide. This often happens even when people are making good progress and moving toward a healthy recovery. As a result, special meetings often arise spontaneously to deal with this event.

If someone announces that he/she has relapsed, the meeting often structures itself around that event, its implications, how the person should relate to the lapse, and so forth. Many participants have the structure of a relapse meeting in the back of their minds and it can be put in operation on a moments notice.

When people relapse, care must be taken so that they do not become so discouraged that they give up on themselves and their program of recovery. While relapse should not be encouraged, easily excused, argued away, or ignored, we all know that most recovering people experience one or more episodes of relapse before their recovery takes hold. As a result, relapse meetings need to walk that thin line between being overly permissive, on the one hand, and harshly judgmental, on the other. In addition, talking about relapse provides an opportunity to underscore how easy it can be to "let one's guard down" and make unwise choices. Thus, a well-orchestrated relapse meeting can comfort the victim and provide a warning to the other attendees.

Concluding Statement

Meetings are an important component of programs of recovery from substance abuse. The benefits of group dynamics can be useful both within a self-help context and within the framework of professional therapy. The tactics used to manage group meetings derive from a variety of sources, including long-established organizations (such as Alcoholics Anonymous and Narcotics Anonymous), the various helping professions, and tools of communication that have been developed by Native people (such as the talking circle method).

In order to provide suggestions regarding how to use group meetings, various suggestions were offered. It is hoped that these ideas will suffice until more tailored methods are developed by those who embrace the Handsome Lake method. Thus, what is stated here should be viewed as elementary suggestions that will need to be expanded on when people employ the Handsome Lake method within their own communities.

PRIVATE SESSIONS: AN OVERVIEW

One-on-one private therapy sessions led by a professional counselor are commonplace in substance abuse therapy. On some occasions, furthermore, one-on-one sessions may involve two lay people; thus AA members often work with a lay sponsor. This kind of nonprofessional private therapeutic relationship has a long tradition in the fight against alcoholism and the results have often been impressive.

THE ALCOHOLICS ANONYMOUS LEGACY

While Alcoholics Anonymous and Narcotics Anonymous are best known for their meetings, the organizations also have a strong tradition of one-on-one interactions and the pairing of two people for their mutual benefit. These therapeutic relationships are best showcased by the organizations' well developed sponsorship program. A basic principle of Alcoholics Anonymous and Narcotics Anonymous is that each member should have a special relationship with a sponsor, who is typically an individual possessing extensive experience in recovery and someone with whom the individual can develop a special relationship.

When an individual is first becoming involved in Alcoholics Anonymous or Narcotics Anonymous, the sponsor is expected to provide the newcomer with counsel, be a special advocate and mentor, and help the novice learn how the program works. In addition, sponsors are expected to be available in case the individual experiences a serious crisis or fears that a relapse is imminent. The whole idea behind the sponsorship relationship is to provide the one-on-one assistance that can help prevent relapse and lead to a healthy and stable recovery. Often sponsors and sponsees spend many hours in places like all night diners and/or hang out together before or after meetings, talking about whatever helps reduce the desire to drink. In the process, they develop a better understanding of the disease while enjoying the fruits of human companionship. Although sponsors and sponsees typically develop a strong bond and friendship, care is taken to insure that the relationship remains therapeutic, at least during the early months of recovery when the threat of relapse is high. As a result, sponsors and sponsees should not be potential sexual partners.

One of the basic principles of Alcoholics Anonymous and Narcotics Anonymous is the assertion that any hidden secret the person holds back may trigger a relapse. As a result, participants are urged to reveal to the sponsor (or to some other person) everything they have done that might be shameful or hurtful. Thus, Alcoholics Anonymous and Narcotics Anonymous clearly affirm that one-on-one relationships are crucial to the program and to long-term sobriety. This is because the program recognizes that people are not willing to broadcast some of their secrets for the whole world to hear.

The influence of Alcoholics Anonymous and Narcotics Anonymous expands beyond the world of self-help because many professional substance abuse counselors are veterans of the Twelve Steps program pattern and their strategy of treatment is patterned around its principles.

THE PROFESSIONAL THERAPY TRADITION

Although many counselors are significantly influenced by the techniques of Alcoholics Anonymous, Narcotics Anonymous, and the Twelve Steps program, they also tend to be impacted by the traditions of the counseling profession. Modern counseling theory and practice strongly emphasize that people often repress what they want to avoid and, thereby, ignore hurtful aspects of their lives in ways that can lead to dysfunction. As a result, the one-on-one counseling relationship provides a forum where these issues can be systematically addressed. Counselors recognize that finding the root of psychological problems can be a long and painful process and that individuals in therapy often need leadership in order to understand themselves and what triggers their dysfunctional behavior. As a result, adjusting therapy to the unique client is a commonplace tactic, even while group therapy is simultaneously employed. On many occasions, however, group activities cannot totally substitute for individual attention; as a result, one-on-one programs deal with the needs of specific clients.

As was discussed above, counseling strategies increasingly acknowledge and respond to cultural differences. Thus, the profession has become actively involved in dealing with diversity and how cultural differences create a need for specific types of therapy that reflect the heritage of the individual.

THE NATIVE AMERICAN RESPECT FOR ELDERS

While the mainstream culture of the United States tends to revolve around youth, many Native people exhibit a special respect for tribal elders: the senior members of society who have mastered their culture and its insights and who seek to transmit these traditions to the next generation. As a result, elders are honored within many Native cultures and occupy a special place in society because of their experience, knowledge, and dedication to their heritage.

Elders are often viewed as master communicators who are able to help people to strengthen themselves and to better understand their cultural legacy even though it may be fragile and under attack. As we saw in earlier chapters, a weakened culture can trigger anxiety and dysfunction. By honoring and learning from elders, some of these negative impacts can be

mitigated. In any event, many Native people honor the bearers of their heritage and they look to them for guidance and leadership. The elders, furthermore, are often careful to interact with other members of the culture in a one-on-one manner in order to preserve the heritage of the people. Thus, many Native people are aware of the value of providing a dialogue regarding their cultural heritage and they are comfortable serving in such a capacity.

DISCUSSION

One-on-one meetings are a valuable tool of therapy. And the methods of one-on-one meetings have roots in self-help tactics, the strategies of the counseling profession, and in Native American traditions. By combining the various techniques available and applying them in relevant ways, an effective formula of intervention can be developed.

SPECIAL TOPICS AND THEIR PURPOSES

A private session may deal with either general or specific issues. As a result, those involved in these meetings can benefit by envisioning an array of ideas that can serve as meeting topics. These concerns can be embraced, as required, in order to serve the needs of those involved. Examples of possible meetings are discussed below.

AN INTRODUCTION TO THE PROGRAM

The Handsome Lake method is new and it will need to be introduced to clients. In order to facilitate this process, a 12-session introduction to the method can be employed. (To save time it might be possible to deal with two steps per meeting and complete the program in 6 weeks.) An example of doing so is discussed in chapter 8 of this book. This 12-session program makes use of the description of the program written for clients (*Recovery the Native Way*) and the consumable workbook. Both of these tools are available from Information Age Publishing.

CULTURAL HERITAGE SESSIONS

A strong cultural heritage is a powerful tool that can help people to mitigate the anxieties they face and deal with the pressures that can trigger dysfunction. On some occasions, particular individuals may have a limited understanding of their culture and/or not perceive the powerful influence it has over them. Thus, on some occasions, one-on-one sessions might focus on general discussions regarding the cultural heritage and its possible impact. In such sessions, individuals can be exposed to a variety of cultural traditions other than their own. The example of Handsome Lake, of course, can be a good starting point for such therapy. In addition, if the individual is a reader, any number of novels about Native American life may prove useful. Especially recommended is N. Scott Momaday's work, especially his novel *House Made of Dawn*. These generic sessions can help individuals to understand the impact of the cultural heritage on their lives and how nurturing and embracing these traditions may provide tools of recovery.

Besides generic discussions that deal with the concept of "cultural heritage" and its importance, individuals often benefit by connecting, in a very personal manner, with their own specific cultural traditions. Many Native peoples have developed a significant literature regarding their cultures. This material should be sought out, if at all possible. Those who deal with a significant number of individuals from the same cultural tradition, may want to assemble their own private library of relevant materials. It is a good idea to have lists of relevant materials that are suitable for people with a variety of reading skills so something will be available for everyone. Therapists who will be dealing with various members of the same cultural group will inevitably become knowledgeable of those traditions. Contacting Native elders or leaders, furthermore, might result in their aid or collaboration. Thus, elders might occasionally "sit in" on a one-on-one meeting, functioning as honored and knowledgeable guests. Those who consider working with elders, or Native healers are strongly encouraged to read Jonathan Ellerby's *Working With Native Elders* (2001) since it gives many valuable perspectives and valuable advice.

CULTURAL STRESS SESSIONS

Cultural stress is a major force impacting the lives of Native people. As the example of Handsome Lake demonstrates, cultural stress (caused by the intrusion of outsiders, economic reversals, disease, etc.) has the ability to undercut people, cause stress, trigger anxiety, and lead to dysfunction. If individuals deal with this reality "head on" in a concrete manner, they may be able to better understand a major force that contributes to their substance abuse.

As with cultural heritage meetings, discussions of cultural stress can be either generic or specific. Besides discussions of Handsome Lake, The work of Harold Napoleon can be a useful tool when initially addressing the stress that faces Native cultures and the dysfunction the resulting anxiety can trigger. When discussions move from general overviews to an analysis of specific cultures and traditions, the discussions need to become focused around the unique history of specific people. Perhaps local histories and the memories of elders can prove to be a valuable point of departure. Maybe clients are well aware of the stresses that are impacting the local culture and it may be possible for them to articulate what has happened to the cultures and the implications of these experiences. In both cases, the discussions can help clients to understand the pressures that are faced and the dysfunction they can trigger.

PATH AND LANDMARK SESSIONS

As with group meetings, the various components of the Path of Handsome Lake and the Landmarks of the Path can be useful topics of discussion Within the context of one-on-one meetings, these topics may be scheduled in advance as required. Since the time available for individual sessions is often severely limited, several or all of the steps and landmarks may be discussed at once. If the individual is attending group sessions, these discussions can be scheduled after the individual has become familiar with these topics, thereby streamlining the process and making more efficient use of one-on-one time.

By doing so, the main issues in the program can be discussed in a manner that makes economical use of the time available while helping individuals to mold the Handsome Lake program around their own individual needs. It can be useful for clients to read the book on the program that has been prepared for them (available from Information Age Publishers.)

Techniques, such as preparing a written exercise to be discussed during the session may help keep sessions focused and, thereby, increase the benefits derived from meetings. You are encouraged to consider using the workbook that is designed to channel writing in positive and focused directions.

These meetings can reinforce the essence of the program and help individuals to understand how the program can be an effective part of their personal recovery.

RELAPSE SESSIONS

Relapse is a common occurrence among recovering substance abusers. And if properly managed, relapse can be an important component of the process of recovery. All too often, however, relapse is viewed as a shameful failure and no benefits are derived from reflecting on what happened and why it occurred. Even worse, relapse can undermine the client's confidence and create apathy that can result in a complete breakdown of the client's program of recovery.

If relapse is discussed in terms of the issues and tensions that might have contributed to it, real benefits may ultimately derive from this unfortunate experience. From a Handsome Lake perspective, a key aspect of relapse might be a weakened cultural heritage or the client's alienation from it. Debriefing sessions that analyze the relapse can provide a insights to those who seek recovery. As a result, special sessions that deal with relapse in an organized and thoughtful manner can be invaluable. Those involved in one-on-one meetings need to have a ready plan in mind for dealing with relapse at a moment's notice, because relapse (and when it occurs) cannot be predicted. While no easy excuses should be given, relapse meetings need to go beyond judgmental evaluations and get down to the hard work of understanding how and why people made the choices they did.

A good way to start this discussion is to acknowledge that the relapse may have been triggered by the stress facing the culture and/or the individual's ability to relate to their heritage in a healthy way. Other causes, of course, often exist. Thus, if a romantic relationship ends, people might get drunk as a result. This kind of event might or might not be related to cultural issues.

DISCUSSION

One-on-one sessions are invaluable tools that can profoundly help those who seek to recover from alcoholism. They can be used in both self-help situations and in professional counseling. While group sessions have their values, on many occasions, people need specific and tailored help. One-on-one sessions can provide it.

CONCLUSION

Although the Handsome Lake program has a significant potential, it is new and those who want to use it need practical suggestions on how it can be applied within a therapeutic context. The discussion provided here suggests a number of practical applications that can be used to facilitate the use of the Handsome Lake method as a functioning program of recovery. I hope these ideas will suffice until a "folklore" regarding the programs arises from those who have used this tool of recovery.

Those seeking to recover from substance abuse can be served either by group meetings or by individual one-on-one sessions that employ the Handsome Lake program. Each of these options has both strengths and weaknesses that have been discussed. Strategies for applying the Handsome Lake method were suggested that made use of both options.

Meetings and sessions, furthermore, can be managed either by laymen or professionals. The benefits of both options have been presented. In doing so, a wide variety of options are analyzed in strategic ways.

The discussion provided here is only preliminary and it is merely intended to fill the void that will exist until the program becomes well enough established for other people to develop methods and techniques that facilitate its use in a wide range of contexts. As a result, those who use the program are encouraged to forge new tactics and to share their successes and challenges with others. To be truly effective, methods of dealing with dysfunction (1) need to mesh with the personal style of those who use them and (2) reflect the needs and heritages of those who are involved. Doing so is recommended here.

REFERENCE

Ellerby, J. H. (2001). *Working with Native elders.* Winnipeg, Manitoba, Canada: Native Studies Press, Univeristy of Manitoba.

Momaday, N. Scott. (1968). *House made of dawn.* New York: Harper & Row.

Prologue to Part 3

While new methods certainly need to be developed, they often have trouble becoming accepted. On the one hand, if a method is to be employed clients must first be diagnosed and evaluated in ways that make the method a logical choice. This can cause a problem for methods that are hinged around cultural stress and\or alienation from a cultural heritage because the *Diagnostic and Statistical Manual of Mental Disorders* (*DSM-IV*) as it now exists makes such a diagnosis very difficult.

Chapters 5 and 6 deal with this issue. Chapter 5 provides a detailed discussion of how and why the *DSM-IV* needs to be revised to deal with cultural issues facing Native people. In doing so, the chapter discusses a number of *DSM-IV* categories that are treated in a truncated manner within the *DSM-IV* in order to show that Native people can experience dysfunction when their culture is under attack and/or when they are alienated form it. In view of the fact that many therapists are seeking to fine tune the *DSM-IV*, this chapter is well within the mainstream of therapeutic thought. By using its suggestions, therapists will have an easier time documenting cultural problems facing Native people that can trigger dysfunction.

While Chapter 5 provides a theoretical discussion, chapter 6 is more applied and provides sample diagnoses using a revised *DSM-IV*. Here, the ideas developed in chapter 5 are applied in real life situations. It is hoped this discussion will prove useful as you employ a broadened *DSM-IV* when evaluating Native clients.

A problem often faced by counselors involves demonstrating to agencies and funding sources exactly how the Handsome Lake program will be implemented. In order to deal with this important issue, chapter 7 provides sample treatment plans for both individuals and groups. They are phrased in a manner that is typical in today's world of greater documentation and accountability. Although your personal style and documentation requirements might require a different format, it is hoped that these examples demonstrate how the Handsome Lake method can be justified and implemented.

Chapter 5

Adjusting the *DSM-IV-TR* to the Needs of Natives

INTRODUCTION

As has often been observed, the *Diagnostic and Statistical Manual of Mental Disorders (DSM-IV-TR)* published by the American Psychiatric Association (2000),[1] is inadvertently culture bound (Eisenbruch, 1992; Fabrega, 1992). As a living and evolving document, however, the *DSM* is constantly being revised in positive, constructive, and equitable ways.

Researchers are striving to expand the *DSM* in an appropriate and relevant manner. In this regard, Novins, Bechtold, Sack, Thompson, and Carter (1997) seek to adjust the *DSM* in order to "assist the clinician in considering the impact that ethnicity and culture may have on the expression of mental illness, it assessment and subsequent treatment" (1997, p. 1244).

Continuing this discussion, Dana has observed "a cultural axis for the DSM could present an emic [client's] perspective from the standpoint of the patient and cultural reference group" (n.d., p. 16.) Thus, as therapists become more aware of the impact of ethnicity and culture on dysfunction, appropriate expansions of the *DSM* are being suggested. This chapter is written in this tradition of positive and constructive adjustments of the *DSM* so it can better serve Native people.

Thus far, most efforts designed to expand the *DSM*'s cultural and ethnic perspectives have dealt with the distinctiveness of specific traditions and the impacts that these differences exert on dysfunction and its diagnosis. The editors emphasize "Special efforts have been made in the preparation of the *DSM-IV* to incorporate an awareness that the manual is used in culturally diverse populations in the United States and internationally" (American Psychiatric Association, 2000 pp. xxxiii-iv).

While these efforts deserve to be applauded, another significant issue needs to be simultaneously addressed: members of different cultures often face parallel pressures and stressors when they are in contact with the mainstream/dominant world. These similar pressures can channel Native responses in parallel ways even when the cultures themselves, are very different. As a result of this tendency, similarities in dysfunction might result from distinct peoples being subjected to similar hurtful experiences. My discussion deals with that potential and its implications.

In order to address these issues, this chapter expands the discussions of three diagnostic categories that are briefly discussed in the *DSM-IV-TR* including "Bereavement"; 313.82 "Identity Problem", and V62.4 "Acculturation Problem" V62.4. The resulting enlarged discussions of these categories provide new and more robust ways to diagnosis a variety of Native dysfunctions (including substance abuse) that are triggered by hurtful contact with the outside world.

BEREAVEMENT AND CULTURAL DECLINE

The *DSM* category of bereavement (V62.8 2) typically deals with dysfunctions that are triggered by the loss of a loved one. The diagnosis of bereavement, as presented in the *DSM*, focuses on the impact triggered by the loss of a specific individual. The diagnosis, for example, reads in part, "This category can be used when the focus of clinical attention is a reaction to the death of a [specific] loved one" (p. 740). Within the mainstream society, envisioning bereavement in this manner might be adequate since the most profound losses many people experience involve the death of a specific person.

Many people are troubled by such a loss. While a specific death is often traumatic and although it can lead to dysfunction, a person's total life is not usually completely swept away by the loss. While people may correctly sense that the death of a dearly loved companion denies them important aspects of life, their world goes on and it often provide support and comfort in troubling times.

These personal losses can be juxtaposed with the grief Native people often experience as their entire way of life is racked by disruptive change or even cultural extinction. To get a taste of this trauma, it is worthwhile to read Theodora Kroeber's *Ishi* (1960). This book is the story of the last remaining member of a Native culture that was completely killed off in the early twentieth century. Looking at Ishi's ordeal, the reader can begin to empathize with the pain faced by those whose entire world had ceased to exist. Although the trauma faced by Ishi was particularly extreme, many Native peoples (and their individual members) have been subjected to a profound dismantling of their cultures and traditions. This process, often labeled "cultural genocide," can exert profound psychological impacts capable of triggering dysfunction, such as substance abuse. Disciplines, such as applied anthropology, have long recognized the hurtful impacts of such trauma. Long ago, for example, G. N. Appell analyzed what he calls the "social separation syndrome ... [that] involves role conflict and ambiguity, threat to one's self-esteem, and an

impaired social identity" (Appell, 1977, p. 14). Appell continues:

> Social bereavement arising from social change seems to follow a developmental sequence similar to personal bereavement.... There is first a period of denial as numbness accompanied by anxiety, fear, and feelings of threat to one's identity. This is succeeded by a phase of frustrated searching for the lost world or individual, hoping for a reversal and then bitter pining and unrelieved sense of pain.... Following this is a period of depression and apathy.... Finally there is the phase of reorganization when the bereaved begins to build new plans and assumptions about the world. (p. 14)

It is important to observe that just as Appell notes parallels between the "social separation syndrome" and other forms of bereavement, the collective and social nature of this phenomena sets it apart from more individual losses (such as the death of a particular loved one.) Appell, incidentally, believes that maintaining the culture as a going concern can be an antidote that protects people from dysfunction. Thus:

> A society undergoing change ... has a right to access to its cultural traditions, its language and its social history. (Appell, 1977, p. 14)

The amount of space available here, of course, prevents a full examination of the theory and method of applied anthropology. As indicated above, however, anthropologists have long noted how trauma and dysfunction are often triggered by profound social change.

Unless the diagnostic category of bereavement is expanded to deal with such broad-based cultural losses, furthermore, other, less precise, diagnostic categories will, by default, be used to deal with the trauma and dysfunction that are triggered by cultural decline. In his widely acclaimed *Yuyaruq: The Way of Being Human*, for example, Harold Napoleon (1996) discusses a wide variety of dysfunctional behaviors, including substance abuse, among Native Alaskans in terms of posttraumatic stress disorder (American Psychiatric Association 2000 category 309.81 pp 463+).

Given the current state of the art of the *DSM IV-TR* (i.e. its truncated treatment of bereavement), Napoleon's use of the posttraumatic stress disorder diagnosis is understandable and useful. Nonetheless, envisioning dysfunction using a broader model that deals with cultural losses (as Appell does) is more elegant, descriptive, and appropriate. In addition, this method of analysis has a long history and cross-disciplinary support.

When considering Appell's work, it becomes clear that the diagnostic category of "bereavement," as articulated in the *DSM IV-TR*, is not adequate in various situations involving Native people. By expanding this category so that it can deal with a number of specific circumstances, "bereavement" becomes a more effective category for diagnosing dysfunction among Native people. For present purposes, it is worthwhile to expand "bereavement" into four distinct, but interrelated categories. They include: (1) Bereavement for an individual; (2) Bereavement for the loss of a group; (3) Bereavement for the loss of a way of life; (4) Bereavement due to the loss of a person's niche in society. Each of these expanded categories will be briefly discussed. (The "SC" designation used in the discussion below stands for "suggested category" that can be used to expand the *DSM IV-TR*.)

BEREAVEMENT FOR AN INDIVIDUAL V62.82 SC 1

The term "bereavement," as presented in the *DSM-IV-TR*, concerns the loss of a particular individuals, typically due to death. This category largely parallels the entire "bereavement" category (V62.82) that occurs in the *DSM-IV-TR* (pages 740-1). People are often traumatized by the loss of a particular person. And this bereavement can trigger dysfunction.

BEREAVEMENT FOR THE LOSS OF A GROUP V62.82 SC 2

As Appell indicates, however, other types of bereavement clearly exist. According to the "social separation syndrome," people often grieve when their culture is destroyed or when they are cut off from it. And this type of bereavement is similar in many ways to the process of grieving for a particular loved one, but it is broader in scope. This type of grieving is typically deeper and more unrelenting because people cannot escape their loss by immersing themselves in their culture or heritage in order to

compensate for their loss (a coping strategy that is often employed in the mainstream world.)

BEREAVEMENT FOR THE LOSS OF A WAY OF LIFE V62.82 SC3

When a Native culture comes in contact with the outside world, not only is the culture placed under great stress, traditional vocations and lifestyles are often undermined. In Alaska, for example, many Native people traditionally practiced a subsistence/ hunting and gathering lifestyle and some members of the Native population still do. In recent decades, however, this traditional way of life has largely disappeared and many people have relocated to urban areas (and are unable to practice a subsistence lifestyle). This destruction of an age-old way of life (and/ or people being denied access to it) has proved to be very traumatic to many Native people. The resulting sorrow and disorientation often triggers dysfunction such as substance abuse.

BEREAVEMENT DUE TO THE LOSS OF A PERSON'S NICHE IN SOCIETY V62.82 SC

In many cases, cultural change that is triggered by outside forces redefines Native society in ways that undercut the traditional roles of certain people. In many Native societies, specific people (such as elders) have traditionally been highly respected and influential individuals. Due to social change triggered by contact, however, the status and pivotal place of such people has often declined or at least been significantly transformed. While skilled hunters are well respected within subsistence communities, for example, when hunting ceases to be a major economic activity, the status associated with a hunter's prowess may fade. People who are nested within the old ways often feel grief as their position within society atrophies. Such sorrow can trigger dysfunctional behavior, such as substance abuse.

Thus, by expanding the concept of bereavement into four distinct categories, it becomes possible to use this category in more refined, descriptive, and useful ways (see Table 5.1).

As cultures decline and/or as they are profoundly transformed, people grieve. This grief can lead to dysfunctional behavior, such as substance abuse. By

Table 5.1.   Bereavement: An Expanded Perspective

Identification	Description	Discussion
V62.82 SC 1	Loss of a specific person, typically a loved one, causes profound sorrow.	This category is similar to the existing "bereavement" category and deals with responses to the death of a specific person.
V62.82 SC 2	The loss of a group or a collective entity is bereaved.	This category is largely parallel to Appell's "social separation syndrome" and refers to the grief felt when the culture, as an entity, declines or is otherwise unavailable to the individual.
V62.82 SC 3	The loss of a way of life is bereaved.	Outside contact and social change often trigger changes in lifestyles and vocational opportunities. These changes can be traumatic and can be grieved by specific individuals.
V62.82 SC 4	The loss of a person's niche in society causes sorrow.	Due to social change, a culture may survive, but the role or niche of specific people may change in hurtful ways. These losses are often grieved by those who are negatively impacted.
Discussion	As articulated in the DSM IV-TR, bereavement deals with the loss of a specific person (typically due to death). Native people, however, often experience other types of bereavement due to cultural change, evolving lifestyles, and transforming statuses. By acknowledging these responses, a more robust envisioning of bereavement is presented.	

expanding our understanding of bereavement, a more robust means of dealing with the problems facing many Native people (and the dysfunctions thereby triggered) can be created. The expanded typology of bereavement presented here is more precise and appropriate than the current formulation of bereavement that exists in the *DSM-IV-TR*. It is also superior to other categories of diagnosis that exist in the *DSM-IV-TR* (such as post-traumatic stress disorder) that have sometimes been used to deal with the bereavement triggered by cultural stress, decline, and extinction.

IDENTITY PROBLEMS AND CULTURAL CONFUSION

A second series of problems centers on personal identity. In the *DSM-IV-TR*, the discussion of identity problems is very generalized and limited to a mere three lines of text. Identity problems are basically defined as "clinical attention ... relating to identity" (American Psychiatric Association, 1980, p. 741). Very little clarification or discussion is provided and only a

bare-bones category is provided. Here, three specific causes and variants of identity problems are presented that may relate to Native people and their dysfunctional behavior. This listing and their subsequent discussions are in no way meant to be exhaustive and it needs to be expanded to deal with the realities of Native life. Although a limited, preliminary formulation, it is hoped that these discussions will be useful, illustrative, and form a foundation for a richer and more appropriate future analysis.

Three specific identity problems to be considered include (1) situations where people are coerced to adjust their identity in order to satisfy the wishes or agendas of others (who may be either Natives or non-Natives), (2) confusion regarding roles and identities that result from an incongruity between different cultural traditions to which the individual has been exposed, and (3) conflicting values that result when a person is simultaneously impacted by the mores of two (or more) cultural traditions. (The "SC" designation used in the discussions stands for "suggested category" that can be used to expand the *DSM IV-TR*.)

COERCION 313.82 SC 1

On many occasions, identity problems result when a specific cultural heritage is forced on people against their will. One particularly damaging variant of this problem took place when mainstream educators attempted to force their culture on Native American students during the "boarding school era" of the United States. In this case, the dominant culture exerted strong efforts that were designed to force Native students to reject their cultural heritage. This process has long been recognized as being a particularly traumatic process that triggered dysfunctional behavior among many former students (even though the problems typically presented themselves years later.) Many Native people who are alumni of the boarding school system (now middle aged or elderly) were hurtfully impacted by this type of coercive dominance. The "alpha variant" will deal with dysfunction that results from the process of the dominant culture attempting to strip people of their Native culture.

The opposite situation is also possible. On some occasions, a person who has been largely acculturated to the mainstream culture might have their Native culture forced on them. Since these people largely identify with the mainstream culture, this can also be a type of cultural coercion that can lead to dysfunction. The "beta variant" deals with such situations.

CONFUSION 313.82 SC 2

When people exist within two different cultures, they may become confused regarding what is proper or inappropriate as well as what is right for them. This situation can be troubling and lead to dysfunctional behavior, such as substance abuse.

CONFLICTING VALUES 313.82 SC 3

The Native and the mainstream cultures often have values that are in conflict with each other. Thus, the mainstream culture embraces the modern world, its culture, priorities and way of life while many Native cultures emphasize traditions and local concerns. As a result, a Native person can be caught between different worlds that have competing priorities, beliefs, ethics, and so forth. This situation can lead to dysfunctional behavior.

Contemporary novelist Philip Roth's novel *Goodbye Columbus* (1994) can be used as an illustrative example of this tendency even though he wrote about Jewish New Yorkers in the twentieth century. The story depicts a community where some people think of themselves as Jewish immigrants and they treasure their religion and their ethnic heritage as well as the close-knit relationships with others that their identity nurtures. Other Jewish New Yorkers, in contrast, may and be proud of their heritage, but think of themselves primarily as Americans (who happen to possess a specific religions and cultural tradition.) Those who are caught between these conflicting values can easily face crises and tensions that can result in dysfunctional responses.

The same sort of tensions that are present in Roth's novel often impact Native cultures and their members. Specific individuals have different values, loyalties, and strategies of life that might trigger conflicts that lead to stress. As a result, many Native people face such a "double bind" that can lead to dysfunctional behavior such as substance abuse.

Thus, just like bereavement, identity problems are complex and multidimensional. Our nonexhaustive typology provides suggestive clues regarding how this category needs to be expanded in order to deal with the pressures faced by Native people. Graphically, these categories and their differences appear as:

Identity crises and cultural confusion can occur in a number of ways. The resulting tensions can result in dysfunction. Due to this reality, a more subtle understanding of identity and cultural confusion is valuable when diagnosing dysfunction among members of the Native community.

ACCULTURATION

In the *DSM IV-TR*, acculturation is discussed in a very brief (2 line) commentary. In a nutshell, acculturation involves "a problem involving adjustment to a different culture" (American Psychiatric Association, 1980, p. 741).

Given the abbreviated analysis, very little clarification or discussion is provided that can be used when conducting an assessment. Here, three specific causes and variants of acculturation problems (as they relate to Native people) are discussed. In one case, the per-

Table 5.2.   Identity and Cultural Confusion: An Expanded Perspective

	Description	*Discussion*
313.82 SC 1	People are coerced into embracing a specific cultural identity in ways that lead to or trigger dysfunction.	The "alpha" variant involves the mainstream culture forcing itself upon a Native person. The "beta" variant involves forcing a person who has been acculturated to the mainstream to practice Native traditions. Both can trigger dysfunction
L313.82 SC 2	People face confusion because they simultaneously exist within multiple cultures or subcultures. The resulting ambiguity can lead to identity problems and a general bewilderment regarding how to think, act, etc. This situation can trigger dysfunction	A person's culture provides most of the basic rules and strategies of life. Furnishing unambiguous roles, beliefs, strategies of response, the culture provides comfort and stability. But when people are simultaneously members of more than one culture, confusion can develop and as a catalyst for dysfunction.
313.82 SC 3	Different cultures have conflicting values. Dealing with these conflicts can lead to pain and crisis and result in dysfunction among some individuals.	Different cultures are often in significant conflict with each other. As a result, people who are members of more than one culture will face crises because their conflicting beliefs and values cannot be easily accommodated. This can lead to an emotional crisis that can trigger dysfunction
Discussion	Culture provides personal identities. And identities are crucial building blocks of personality, adaptation, and response. Possessing multiple identities can cause confusion and conflict. When these stresses exist and when they are not mitigated, people can become vulnerable to dysfunctional behavior, such as substance abuse.	

son has trouble interacting within the Native culture. In another, the person has trouble interacting within the mainstream world. And finally, some individuals may have trouble interacting both within the Native and the mainstream culture. These variants may not be exhaustive and many other examples and categories could easily be developed. It is hoped, however, that these discussions will prove useful and illustrative. (The "SC" designation used in the discussions stands for "suggested category" that can be used to expand the *DSM IV-TR*.)

INABILITY TO FUNCTION IN NATIVE CULTURE V62.2 SC 1

Many Native people have a strong emotional need to identify with and interact within their traditional culture, but they lack the ability to do so. This incapacity may result from a wide variety of causes. Some

people have only minimal knowledge of their heritage. Thus, many Native people lament the fact that they do no know how to speak their Native language, lack a basic understanding of their Native culture's beliefs, customs, and so forth. As a result, these people may be cut off from an important aspect of themselves (and/or feel that they are hurtfully alienated from something that is important to them.)

On other occasions, individuals may possess the knowledge required to interact within their Native culture but, for some reason, be unable to do so. Many individuals, for example, live away from other Native people and/or have no Native cohorts with whom to interact.)

The inability to function within a Native culture and/or feelings of alienation from the Native culture can exert powerful negative influences capable of triggering dysfunctional behavior, such as substance abuse.

INABILITY TO FUNCTION IN MAINSTREAM CULTURE V62.4 SC 2

In some cases, a person may lack an ability to function adequately within the mainstream culture. This situation can undercut the ability to be "successful" in life. This inability can also lead to problems of lowered self-esteem. Those who identify with the mainstream culture may be particularly traumatized by this situation. Dysfunctional behavior may result.

INABILITY TO FUNCTION IN ANY CULTURE V62.4 SC 3

Some individuals may be caught between two different cultural spheres and not be skilled, comfortable, or accepted in either. People in this situation are particulary vulnerable. Table 5.3 compares the acculturation problems.

Bereavement, identity problems, and acculturation problems, therefore, are three key issues that can create trauma in Native people and trigger dysfunction.

While these three categories exist within the *DSM-IV-TR*, each is only discussed in the briefest of ways there. To compensate for the briefness of the discussions in the *DSM-IV-TR*, each category is significantly expanded so they can more effectively deal with Native people and the dysfunctional behaviors they exhibit. While these discussions are in not exhaustive, it is hoped that they will be useful and encourage additional thought regarding how the *DSM-IV-TR* can be expanded in order to deal with the particular problems faced by Native people.

APPLICATIONS

This book agrees with the commonly stated observation that the *DSM-IV-TR* is inadvertently culture bound and, as a result, its use might distort the diagnoses of people who are not products of the industrialized West. While some researchers seek to expand the *DSM-IV* to deal with specific cultures, this

Table 5.3.   Acculturation Problems: An Expanded Perspective

	Description	*Discussion*
V62.2 SC 1	Inability to function within the Native culture of origin	Some Native people lack an ability to function effectively within their traditional culture. These people, for example, are often unable to speak their Native language and/or understand subtle aspects of their culture and how it works. Others have no Native cohorts and are unable to participate in their culture for this reason. These situations can be troubling and can lead to dysfunction.
V62 SC 2	Inability to function within the mainstream culture	Some Native people have not adequately mastered the mainstream culture and/or are not accepted by it. This situation can lead to reduced cultural opportunities and/or self-esteem problems that can trigger dysfunction. This situation can be particularly troubling to those who identify with the mainstream culture.
V62.2 SC 3	Multiple acculturation problems	The individual lacks the skills needed to interact effectively both within the Native and mainstream cultures and/or are accepted in neither cultural arena.
Discussion	People who must exist in more than one cultural context often find themselves to be handicapped within one or both social contexts. These situations can trigger dysfunctional behavior such as substance abuse.	

approach suggests that a wide variety of Native cultures are impacted by the outside world in parallel ways. These categories of the *DSM-IV-TR* are expanded so they can be more useful when diagnosing Native people.

People from different cultures who are negatively impacted in similar ways may develop similar patterns of dysfunction, even if these cultures are not closely related. Here, relevant categories of the *DSM-IV-TR* have been expanded in order to more effectively deal with a wide range of Native people. They include "Bereavement" (V62.82), "Identity Problem" (313.82), and "Acculturation Problem" (V62.4.) By developing more robust categories, the process of diagnosing and treating Native dysfunction can be enhanced.

A EXPANDED TOOL OF DIAGNOSIS

As we are all aware, diagnosis precedes treatment. And the specific diagnosis typically suggests the type of treatment that will be prescribed.

This situation has created a "Catch 22" that has worked against the best interests of many Native people seeking recovery. As the *DSM-IV-TR* currently exists, the categories of "Bereavement," "Identity Problem," and "Acculturation Problem" are not robust enough to adequately deal with a variety of problems that afflict many Native people. Due to the limits of the current *DSM* categories, an adequate and appropriate diagnosis can become impossible. When this occurs, Native people seeking treatment may not be adequately served.

In order to deal with this problem, I have shown how a number of categories that exist in truncated form within the *DSM-IV-TR* can be expanded in useful ways that continue the spirit of the *DSM* category, on the one hand, while facilitating a more appropriate assessment of Native clients on the other.

In recent years, the *DSM* project (as an ongoing entity) has made important strides by acknowledging

cultural relativity and by working its perspectives into the diagnosis of dysfunctional behavior. My work is a part of this tradition and it seeks to enhance the relevance of that important document. I hope that my discussions will help therapists grapple with issues concerning how to portray cultural stress in a manner that embraces the *DSM IV-TR*, on the one hand, while adequately serving the needs of Native clients, on the other.

NOTE

1. As well as earlier and future versions.

REFERENCES

American Psychiatric Association. (2000). *Diagnostic and statistical manual of mental disorders* (DSM-IV-TR). Washington, DC: Author.

Appell, G. N. (1977). The plight of indigenous people: Issues and dilemmas. *Survival International Review, 2*(3), 11-16.

Dana, R. H. (n.d.) Examining the usefulness of DSM-IV. Manuscript draft of chapter 3 for Kurasaki, K. Okazzaki, S, and Sue S. (Eds). *Asian American Mental Health: Assessment, Theories and Methods.*

Eisenbruch, M. (1992). Toward a culturally sensitive *DSM*: Cultural bereavement in Cambodian refugees and the traditional healer as taxonomist. *Journal of Nervous and Mental Disease, 180*, 8-10.

Fabrega, H. (1992). Diagnosis interminable: Towards a culturally sensitive DSM-IV. *Journal of Nervous and Mental Disease, 180*, 5-7

Kroeber, T. (1960). *Ishi.* Berkeley: University of California Press.

Napoleon, H. (1996). *Yuyaruq: The way of being human.* Fairbanks: Alaska Native Knowledge Network.

Novins, D. K., Bechtold, D. W., Sack, W. H., Thompson, J., Carter, D. R. (1997). The DSM-IV outline for cultural formation: A critical demonstration with American Indian children. *Journal of American Academy of Child and Adolescent Psychiatry, 36*(9), 1244-1251.

Roth, P. (1994). *Goodbye Columbus.* New York: Vintage.

Chapter 6

The Process and Strategies of Diagnosis

INTRODUCTION

As suggested in chapter 6, the process of diagnosing a variety of dysfunctions triggered by cultural stress and/or cultural alienation is very difficult when using the standard *DSM-IV* scheme of evaluation. This is because the *DSM-IV* reflects findings gleaned from the mainstream population, not distinctive niches of people, such as Native populations. Currently, however, an important research stream seeks to broaden the applicability of the DSM in order for it to more meaningfully deal with a wider range of individuals.

Chapter 6 suggests ways in which the *DSM-IV* can be adjusted to better reflect the trauma and dysfunction faced by Native people. In specific, three categories of diagnosis that the *DSM-IV* considers in an abbreviated form were expanded in order to meaningfully deal with the reality of Native life and the needs of Native clients. They include the categories of "Bereavement" (V 62.8.2), "Identity Problem" (313.82), and "Acculturation Problem" (V 62.2).

These categories were expanded and refined with reference to the traumas that Native people often face. As a result, more precise and refined categories are made available to those who deal with Native clients.

EXAMPLES OF USING THESE EXPANDED CATEGORIES

While proposing addendums to the *DSM-IV* is an interesting intellectual exercise, those in the practitioner world need advice regarding how to apply them in actual diagnoses and evaluations. In this chapter, the popular "SOAP" format of diagnosis and assessment is used to demonstrate how to do so. The SOAP model (which breaks the analysis/assessment down into four categories—Subjective statements, Objective observations, Assessment, and Plan) is so well known that it hardly needs a detailed discussion here. Nonetheless, as a courtesy to the reader, sample SOAP diagnoses are provided below. In order for the reader to be somewhat familiar with the particular example being offered, my initial SOAP analysis/assessment is based on the old Townes Van Zant song "Pancho and Lefty" made famous by Willy Nelson. The SOAP analysis/assessment of Pancho is presented in Table 6.1.

I do not use this scheme because I want to urge others to follow my example. I merely employ the SOAP method as a didactic devise that is well known and can be usefully employed here. Professional therapists, of course, have their own preferences of assessment and documentation and various agencies have their specific required formats that must be followed.

Table 6.1.   SOAP Analysis/Assessment

Pancho

Subjective	Pancho states he lives a charmed life because of his prowess. He boasts that he wears his gun outside of his pants for all the world to fear. He recalls that long ago he thought that living on the road would make him free and clean, but now admits that he has come to wear his skin like iron and that his breath smells like kerosene. And yet, he brags, his horse is like polished steel. And nobody can touch him. He has many stories of his daring do. And they portray him as invincible.
Objective	The Federales (Mexican federal police) said they could have caught him any day. They only let him slip away out of kindness, I suppose.
Assessment	Pancho has developed unrealistic attitudes and beliefs regarding his ability to control the situation. He might be trusting people who he should be wary of. He's taking dangerous risks and when the law catches up with him the situation will be very serious.
Plan	Pancho needs to assess his current lifestyle and its risks. I need to help him plan for assessing the risks he is taking and their implications. Since his unrealistic feelings of invincibility may stem from alcohol or drug use, efforts should be taken to assess his drinking and drugging and their impacts. Since Pancho is not mandated to participate, however, I have little leverage over him.

Nonetheless, I hope that these discussions provide a better understanding regarding how to make more focused diagnoses and evaluations that involve cultural issues.

The presentation of this chapter employs the categories and subcategories of the *DSM-IV* that were expanded in chapter 6 by using a SOAP method analysis. In this way, the reader will see how these expanded categories can be used to evaluate clients and document their needs.

BEREAVEMENT

The term "Bereavement" in the *DSM* is very truncated and seemingly refers almost exclusively to the loss of a loved one, typically through death. When people lose their culture or their place in their culture, however, they can also feel bereavement. Unfortunately, unless the category of Bereavement is expanded, a number of diagnoses and evaluations cannot be made using the *DSM* schema. Here Bereavement is expanded into four discrete categories.

V 62.82 SC1: "Loss of a specific person, typically a loved one, causes profound sorrow." This category basically embodies the entire category of bereavement as it appears in the *DSM-IV.* A sample assessment could be, *"The client is extremely*

disturbed and distraught due to the death of her husband. This fits the criteria of V 62.82 SC1 in the *DSM-IV."*

V 62.82 SC2: "The loss of a group or collective entity is bereaved." On many occasions, Native cultures evolve in ways that shrink the community and/or destroy certain aspects of it. When this happens people may grieve. A sample assessment may be *"The client is grieving because his small village in interior Alaska was abandoned and the people dispersed. He misses that environment and is saddened because it no longer exists.* This evaluation fits the criteria of V 62,82 SC2."

V 62.82 SC3: "The loss of a way of life is bereaved." Due to rapid cultural change, many ways of life are disappearing and/or fewer people are able to practice them. This situation can have a traumatic impact on some Native people. A sample assessment might be, *"The client formally lived a subsistence lifestyle of hunting and fishing but has had to give it up. This situation is causing the client to feel significant grief."* This evaluation fits the criteria of V 62.82 SC3."

V 62.82 SC4: "The loss of a person's niche in society causes sorrow." People in a Native society may lose their niche in society as times and circumstances change. This can make people unhappy. A sample assessment might be, *"The client has long* *been an elder in a remote village and in that role was a respected leader. She has had to move to Fairbanks, Alaska for health reasons and can no longer fulfill the elder's role. This grieves her.* This evaluation fits the criteria of V 62. 82 SC4."

IDENTITY AND CULTURAL CONFUSION

For a variety of reasons and in a number of ways, people can suffer from identity and cultural confusion. The *DSM-IV* collapses various types of this response into one category. When dealing with Native populations, the category can be usefully expanded. Here, three more precise categories are suggested.

313.82SC 1: "People are coerced into embracing a specific cultural identity in ways that lead to or trigger dysfunction."

Alpha variant: "Mainstream culture forced on Native person." On some occasions, a mainstream way of life is forced on a Native person. This can be very painful. A sample assessment might be *"The client was sent to boarding school outside of his village as a young boy and denied his culture. This has caused much confusion and sorrow that has led to alcoholic drinking.* The client is experiencing 313.82 SC1 Alpha of the DSM-IV."

Beta Variant: "Native identity is forced on someone who prefers the mainstream culture." On some occasions, a client may be a Native person who prefers the mainstream culture and has been acculturated to it, but is forced to live a Native lifestyle. This situation can be traumatic. An example might be, *"The client spent many years in Fairbanks, Alaska and identifies with the mainstream culture. His family has recently relocated to a Native village located off the road network. The young man is very depressed and is drinking heavily.* The client is experiencing 313.82 SC1 of the DSMIV."

313.82SC2: "People face confusion because they simultaneously exist within multiple cultures or subcultures. The resulting ambiguity can lead to identity problems and a general bewilderment regarding how to think, act, etc. This situation can trigger dysfunction." Many Native people have a foot in both worlds and they may have trouble deciding where they belong or where their loyalties lie. An example assessment might be, *"The client does not know where she belongs. She has equally strong connections to the Native and the mainstream cultures and, as a result, she faces constant conflicts.* This client is experiencing 313.82 SC3 of the DSM-IV."

313.82SC3: "Different cultures have conflicting values. Dealing with these conflicts can lead to pain and crisis and result in dysfunction among some individuals." When people live within two different cultures they often face conflicting values. If these issues are not resolved and/or if priorities are not set, unhappiness can result. A sample assessment might be, *"The client is a good worker with a bright future who loves his Native heritage. His family expects him to go to fish camp and Moose hunting, but doing so will anger his boss in Anchorage, Alaska and disappoint his girlfriend. There is no way in which he can please everybody and he is becoming increasingly depressed.* The client is experiencing 313.82. SC3 of the DSM-IV."

ACCULTURATION

Acculturation in the *DSM-IV* is a blanket term. It refers to the ability to function within a specific cultural milieu. The term needs to be expanded because some Native people have trouble functioning within their Native culture while others have trouble within the mainstream culture. And some unfortunate people have trouble functioning in both. Each of these three categories needs to be recognized.

V62.2 SC1: "Inability to function within the Native Culture of Origin." Some Native people lack the skills and abilities they need to function within their Native culture. Various people who attended boarding schools, for example, grieve because they cannot speak their Native language. When people cannot function within their Native group, they often feel isolated, lonely, unworthy, and depressed. A sample diagnosis might be, *"The client is a young woman who left her village after high* *school and went to college. She earned a degree and is doing very well professionally. Nonetheless, she is unhappy because she has been away so much she has trouble interacting within her community. She is suffering from V62.2 SC I of the DSM-IV."*

V62.2 SC2: "Inability to function within mainstream culture." Some Native people may feel badly because they are not able to function within the mainstream culture. This can trigger problems. A sample evaluation might be, *"The client lives in Fairbanks, Alaska, but was raised in a small village off the road network He has not been in Fairbanks very long and is very disoriented by living in a large community dominated by non-Natives. This is causing problems and his drinking is increasing. He is suffering from V62. 2 SC3."*

V62.2 SC3: "Multiple acculturation problems." Some Native people may have trouble interacting within both the mainstream and the Native culture. This can lead to trauma. A sample evaluation might be, *"The client is half Native and half White. He has lived on and off both in an Alaska Native community and in the "lower 48." He does not feel he belongs*

Table 6.2.   A Sample of a Culturally Sensitive Evaluation

Woodstock

Subjective	Woodstock states that over the years she has gotten to be a "big city chick." She tells me that she is different from a lot of those Native girls who have never been "out of the sticks." And this young woman affirms that she certainly doesn't want to be lumped together with such boring village people. She tells me that she finds village life to be atrocious. She said doesn't want to live in a village off the road system, but that is where her family is. She told stories about going to New York State and seeing a lot of famous rock and roll bands.
Objective	Woodstock is pregnant and "showing." She already has one young child. The infant appears to be part White. She is very well dressed except for a well-worn T-shirt that is a souvenir of the 25th anniversary Woodstock restaging that was held in 1994. It appeared that she is wearing this threadbare old rag in order to demonstrate that she's "been around" and not lived all her life in small Alaskan villages. It was as if this shirt validated and affirmed her; why else would she be nicely dressed except for a worn out T-shirt? She is with a female cousin, who is attractive. The cousin in not currently pregnant, but does have two small children. Woodstock has a never-ending array of stories about the exciting things she has done. She gently "puts down" her cousin for being a country bumpkin.
Assessment	Woodstock seems to be alienated from the rural life of Native Alaskans. She seems unfulfilled and unhappy about being back "up North." She views herself as a Lower 48/big city girl, who is stuck in Alaska with a young child and another on the way. She keeps clinging to her image and to the memories of the past (or, perhaps, her fantasias of the past). She does not seem to be ready for her likely fate: life among in a rural Native village with two children to care for and no dependable man in sight. She is at family therapy to talk about Fetal Alcohol Syndrome because she is pregnant. No man came with her, just the female cousin who appears to be a part of her support network. She shows signs of being alienated from these assets. In terms of the DSM-IV, she seems to be suffering from V 62.82 SC3: "The loss of a way of life is bereaved," 313.82 SC 1 Beta variant, "a person acculturated to the mainstream culture is forced to practice Native traditions," and V62.2 SC 1 "an inability to function within the Native culture of origin."
Plan	Woodstock seems vulnerable to alienation from herself, her people, her life, and her future. Given the fact that she has young children, it appears she will be trapped for a long time. This will probably make her very unhappy. There appears to be no "prince charming" on the horizon. Woodstock needs interventions that are designed to help her cope with the situation she faces. She needs to figure out how to make the most of her life. She needs to adjust. She needs to feel good about herself and her fate. She needs to find a place for herself. I predict if she doesn't do so, she will become increasingly unhappy and that this unhappiness has the potential to translate itself into a number of possible dysfunctional behaviors.

in either world and is very lonely and unhappy. He is experiencing V62. 2 SC 3 of the DSM-IV."

USEFUL ADDITIONS

Native people often experience emotional trauma and dysfunction because of issues that relate to their cultural heritage. Many of these problems, however, are not frequently seen within the mainstream population and, as a result, the *DSM-IV* has dealt with these categories in an abbreviated manner. Three such categories are "Bereavement", "Identity and Cultural Confusion," and "Acculturation."

In this chapter these expanded categories have are discussed so that client evaluations and assessments can be more precise. By doing so, therapists will be able to better document the needs of their clients and more effectively plan and implement therapeutic interventions.

A SAMPLE OF A CULTURALLY SENSITIVE EVALUATION

As indicated, culturally sensitive evaluations are very important when dealing with Native clients. This chapter is designed to help you to do so. Table 6.2 above is a sample SOAP evaluation in which some of these expansions of *DSM* categories are used in an assessment. I hope it demonstrates ways in which these expanded categories can serve a useful role in evaluating clients and forging treatment plans.

Chapter 7

Sample Treatement Plans

Thus far, this book has presented an array of discussions that are designed to help the therapist envision the Handsome Lake method as a culturally sensitive strategy that can be used when conducting therapy among Native people. In doing so, a unique method of therapy has been provided. In addition, this book has provided discussions regarding how to adjust evaluation and assessment tools (such as the *DSM-IV*) in order to take the distinctiveness of the Native experience into account. Combined these discussions provide a useful tool of value when serving Native clients.

A last issue involves providing real-life examples regarding how to apply the Handsome Lake method in actual therapeutic circumstances. Doing so is accomplished here. My strategy is to present simple treatment plans that employ the Handsome Lake method. To give you flexibility, plans for both (1) individual and (2) group therapy are provided. Invariably, specific therapists will adjust these suggestions to mesh with their own personal style and the unique needs of their clients. Nevertheless, these suggestions provide concrete examples of how the Handsome Lake method can be applied within the context of therapy involving Native clients.

TREATMENT PLAN FOR 12-WEEK THERAPEUTIC RELATIONSHIP WITH

Client Name

Presenting Problem: Alcoholic Dependence DSM IV-TR 303.90
By Alf H. Walle

DEFINITIONS

1. Client exhibits a drinking pattern that can be clinically described as alcoholic.

2. Client feels his relationship to alcohol is influenced by (1) bereavement for a lost of his /her culture/way of life, (2) identity confusion, and (3) acculturation problems.

3. Client states that although he/she wants to stop drinking, he/she has been unable to gain the skills and insights needed to do so from mainstream alcohol abuse therapy and/or mainstream self-help groups with which he/she has been previously involved

---

GOALS

1. Make client aware of the seriousness of alcohol abuse.

2. Help client deal with the issues of bereavement (DSM-IV 62.82), and acculturation problems (DSM-IV 313.82.)

3. Help client believe it is possible to live a good and fruitful life free of alcohol.

4. Help client gain culturally specific tools needed for recovery.

5. Make client aware of culturally sensitive options of therapy and self-help

---

TREATMENT

Date	Objective	Interventions
Session 1	Initial meeting. Help client adjust to and understand treatment. Introduce the degree to which alienation from a culture can inflict pain, even if the person is not overtly aware of the impact	A week before treatment begins the client will be given a copy of *Recovery the Native Way* and the accompanying workbook. In the first meeting, the program of therapy will be introduced and exercises based on chapter 1 will be discussed. This discussion will underscore the pain that may be associated with alienation from one's culture and/or a lack of access to it.
Session 2	Help the client focus on his/her specific Native culture, his/her relationship to it, and the relation it may have to the client's pattern of drinking	Before the session the client will read chapter 2 of *Recovery the Native Way* and complete the accompanying exercises in the workbook. In the session, the client will begin to identify his/her Native culture and his/her relationship to it. The goal is to build a greater self awareness of the client's cultural heritage and its possible impact on alcohol abuse (and hopefully recovery.)

TREATMENT (Continued)

Date	Objective	Interventions
Session 3	The client is introduced to various theories of alcohol abuse involving Native people. The client is asked to think of these theories in terms of his/her own experience.	Before the session the client will read chapter 3 of *Recovery the Native Way* and complete the accompanying exercises in the workbook. Session work will help the client clarify and articulate his/her Native cultural identify and his/her relationship to it.
Session 4	Various theories and programs of alcohol therapy exist. Many of them fail to take the client's specific cultural heritage into account. They also typically fail to deal with the fact that the culture may be under stress and/or that the client may be alienated from their traditions. This session deals with these issues.	Before the session the client will read chapter 4 of *Recovery the Native Way* and complete the accompanying exercises in the workbook. In this session, the client will explore various models of recovery and the fact that few of these methods deal with cultural stress and cultural alienation. The client will address these issues and the degree to which they need to be dealt with.
Session 5	Various theories of social stress and how social stress triggers dysfunction have been developed. The client in introduced to these theories and asked to relate them to his/her life.	Before the session the client will read chapter 5 of *Recovery the Native Way* and complete the accompanying exercises in the workbook. In the session a wide variety of theories regarding social stress and dysfunction will be discussed. In doing so, the client will explore what these theories reveal about his /her life and alcoholic behavior.
Session 6	The case of the nineteenth century Iroquois (Native people of New York State) is introduced. It is shown that the Iroquois exhibited a pattern of cultural stress and dysfunction that parallels many modern Native people.	Before the session the client will read chapter 6 of *Recovery the Native Way* and complete the accompanying exercises in the workbook. The session, will start with a discussion of the Iroquois as an historic example. The discussion will eventually focus upon the fact that the situation faced by the Iroquois appears to be part of a larger pattern that may have parallels in the client's Native culture.
Session 7	The example of Handsome Lake (a nineteenth century Iroquois leader who overcame alcoholism and provided a method for (1) his culture to regroup and (2) for individuals to recovery from alcoholism) is discussed. Parallels to modern Native people are emphasized.	Before the session the client will read chapter 7 of *Recovery the Native Way* and complete the accompanying exercises in the workbook. The session will deal with the fact that recovery is possible and that recovery may be facilitated by focusing on the Native culture and adjusting it to evolving circumstances.
Session 8	The "Path of Handsome Lake" is introduced. It is presented as a culturally sensitive method of recovery that stems from the Native experience.	Before the session the client will read chapter 8 of *Recovery the Native Way* and complete the accompanying exercises in the workbook. In the session the client will deal with the Path of Handsome Lake as a method of therapy that has the potential to deal with alcoholism by focusing on the stress facing the Native culture and the client's relationship to his/her heritage.

TREATMENT (Continued)

Date	Objective	Interventions
Session 9	The "Landmarks of the Path" is introduced. It is presented as a culturally sensitive agenda by which the Path of Handsome Lake method can be applied to therapy and life.	Before the session the client will read chapter 9 of *Recovery the Native Way* and complete the accompanying exercises in the workbook. In the session the Landmarks will be discussed as a method by which the path can be applied in a systematic and productive manner.
Session 10	The value of using the Handsome Lake method in future therapy is discussed. Other issues that are arising can also be discussed.	Before the session the client will read chapter 10 of *Recovery the Native Way* and complete the accompanying exercises in the workbook. In the session, the value of the method in future therapy will be discussed. The client will be able to raise other related issues as required
Session 11	The value of using the Handsome Lake method in a self-help context is discussed. Other issues that are arising can also be discussed.	Before the session the client will read chapter 11 of *Recovery the Native Way* and complete the accompanying exercises in the workbook. In the session, the value of the method in future self-help activities will be discussed. The client will also be able to raise other issues as required.
Session12	Wrap-up. Answer questions, assure client of the availability of future help.	Help the client synthesize what has been learned in ways that can be applied to life and therapy. Make sure client is aware of available support. Congratulate client on a successful program.

TREATMENT PLAN FOR 12 WEEK THERAPEUTIC RELATIONSHIP WITH

An Array of Clients in Group Therapy

Presenting Problem: Alcoholic Dependence *DSM IV-TR* 303.90
By Alf H. Walle

DEFINITIONS

1. The group is composed of an array of clients that exhibit drinking patters that can clinically be described as alcoholic.

2. It appears that the clients feel that their relationship to alcohol is influenced by bereavement for a loss of the culture/way of life, Identity confusion and/or acculturation problems.

3. Clients states that although they wants to stop drinking, they have been unable to gain the skills and insights needed to do so from mainstream alcohol abuse therapy and/or mainstream self-help groups with which they has been previously involved

---

GOALS

1. Make clients aware of the seriousness of alcohol abuse

2. Help clients deal with the issues of bereavement (DSM IV 62.82), and acculturation problems (DSM IV 313.82.)

3. Help clients believe it is possible to live a good and fruitful life free of alcohol.

4. Help clients gain culturally specific tools needed for recovery.

5. Make clients aware of culturally sensitive options of therapy and self-help

---

TREATMENT

Date	Objective	Interventions
Session 1	Initial meeting. Help clients adjust to and understand treatment. Introduce the degree to which alienation from a culture can inflict pain on people, even if they are not overtly aware of the impact.	A week before treatment begins clients will be given copies of *Recovery the Native Way* and the accompanying workbook. In the first meeting, the program of therapy will be introduced and exercises based on chapter 1 will be discussed. This discussion will underscore the pain that may be associated with alienation from one's culture and/or lacking access to it.
Session 2	Help clients to focus on their specific Native cultures, their relationship to them, and the relation cultural identity issues might have on the clients' pattern of drinking.	Before the session clients will read chapter 2 of *Recovery the Native Way* and complete the accompanying exercises in the workbook. In the session, clients will begin to identify their Native culture and their relationship to it. The goal is to build a greater self awareness of the clients' cultural heritage and its possible impact upon alcohol abuse (and hopefully recovery.)

Date	Objective	Interventions
Session 3	Clients are introduced to various theories of alcohol abuse involving Native people. Clients will be asked to think of these theories in terms of their own experiences.	Before the session clients will read chapter 3 of *Recovery the Native Way* and complete the accompanying exercises in the workbook. Session work will help clients clarify and articulate their Native cultural identifies and their relationship to them.
Session 4	Various theories and programs of alcohol therapy exist. Many of them fail to take the clients' specific cultural heritage into account. They also typically fail to deal with the fact that the culture may be under stress and/or that the clients may be alienated from their traditions in some way. This session deals with these issues.	Before the session clients will read chapter 4 of *Recovery the Native Way* and complete the accompanying exercises in the workbook. In this session, clients will explore various models of recovery and the fact that few of these methods deal with cultural stress and cultural alienation. Clients will address these issues and the degree to which they need to be dealt with.
Session 5	Various theories of social stress and how social stress triggers dysfunction have been developed. Clients are introduced to these theories and asked to relate them to their life	Before the session clients will read chapter 5 of *Recovery the Native Way* and complete the accompanying exercises in the workbook. In the session a wide variety of theories regarding social stress and dysfunction will be discussed. In doing so, clients will explore what these theories reveal about their lives and alcohol behavior
Session 6	The case of the nineteenth century Iroquois (Native people of New York State) is introduced. It is shown that the Iroquois exhibited a pattern of cultural stress and dysfunction that parallels many modern Native people.	Before the session clients will read chapter 6 of Recovery *the Native Way* and complete the accompanying exercises in the workbook. The session, will start with a discussion of the Iroquois as an historic example. The discussion will eventually focus on the fact that the situation faced by the Iroquois appears to be part of a larger pattern that may have parallels in the clients' Native cultures.
Session 7	The example of Handsome Lake (a nineteenth century Iroquois leader who overcame alcoholism and provided a method for his culture to regroup and for individuals to recovery from alcoholism) is discussed. Parallels to modern Native people are emphasized.	Before the session clients will read chapter 7 of *Recovery the Native Way* and complete the accompanying exercises in the workbook. The session will deal with the fact that recovery is possible and that recovery may be facilitated by focusing upon the Native culture and adjusting it to evolving circumstances.
Session 8	The "Path of Handsome Lake" is introduced. It is presented as a culturally sensitive method of recovery that stems from the Native experience.	Before the session clients will read chapter 8 of *Recovery the Native Way* and complete the accompanying exercises in the workbook. In the session clients will deal with the Path of Handsome Lake as a method of therapy that has the potential to deal with alcoholism by focusing upon the stress facing the Native culture and the clients' relationship to their heritage.

TREATMENT (Continued)

Date	Objective	Interventions
Session 9	The "Landmarks of the Path" is introduced. It is presented as a culturally sensitive agenda by which the Path of Handsome Lake method can be applied to therapy and life.	Before the session clients will read chapter 9 of *Recovery the Native Way* and complete the accompanying exercises in the workbook. In the session the Landmarks will be discussed as a method by which the path can be applied in a systematic and productive manner.
Session 10	The value of using the Handsome Lake method in future therapy is discussed. Other issues that are arising can also be discussed.	Before the session clients will read chapter 10 of *Recovery the Native Way* and complete the accompanying exercises in the workbook. In the session, the value of the method in future therapy will be discussed. Clients will be able to raise other related issues as required
Session 11	The value of using the Handsome Lake method in a self-help context is discussed. Other issues that are arising can also be discussed.	Before the session clients will read chapter 11 of *Recovery the Native Way* and complete the accompanying exercises in the workbook. In the session, the value of the method in future self-help activities will be discussed. Client will also be able to raise other issues as required.
Session12	Wrap-up. Answer questions, assure clients of the availability of future help	Help clients synthesize what has been learned in ways that can be applied to life and therapy. Make sure clients are aware of available support. Congratulate client on a successful program.

These treatment plans are only presented for illustrative purposes, although therapists who are using the Handsome Lake Program may find helpful clues in what they find above. Each therapist, of course, will adjust the Handsome Lake program and the DSM-IV as required and in ways that fit their professional styles and the requirements of their agencies.

In any event, the Handsome Lake Program provides a useful way to deal with cultural issues that might trigger substance abuse. The program is especially designed to deal with massive social change and its impact on Native cultures as well as the pain that can result from an individual's alienation from his/her heritage. Both of these factors can profoundly impact individuals and lead to dysfunction.

By appropriately adjusting the DSM-IV, issues not otherwise showcased during mainstream diagnosis can be documented. Once recognized, strategies of intervention that embrace the Native culture (such as the Handsome Lake Program) can be proposed and justified.

Conclusion

This book is intended to help substance abuse counselors to more effectively deal with Native clients. I suggest that mainstream programs of therapy often do not adequately deal with a wide array of problems that Native people often face. Significant among these issues is the fact that Native cultures are often under significant attack and they may be declining to the point where they can no longer nurture and protect people. As a result, the culture, traditions, and heritage of the people cannot help people combat their substance abuse. A weakened Native culture, furthermore, is often the catalyst that triggered substance abuse in the first place.

In order to present this argument, relevant reviews of the literature were conducted, an account of a Native-based residential recovery program was provided, and components of the *DSM-IV* were expanded to better deal with Native issues.

Detailed descriptions of The Handsome Lake method, the "Path of Handsome Lake," and the "Landmarks of the Path" were also offered. Practitioner flesh was put on these theoretical bones by providing suggestions for employing the method and providing sample treatment plans.

It is hoped that this book (coupled with the description written for clients and the consumable workbook also available from Information Age Publishing) will prove useful to you and your clients. Good luck.

Appendix

The Path and Landmarks in Poster Form

Those who employ the Handsome Lake method need to reminded of the framework that is provided by the Path and the Landmarks.

In order to make it easier to keep the program in mind, I am providing statements of both of these tools in poster form. It is hoped that those using the program will photocopy these posters and put them in a prominent place so the principles of the program can be kept in mind.

The Path of Handsome Lake

1. I possess a culture and a tradition. Embracing them is sacred, meaningful, and joyful.

2. All cultural traditions change and all cultural traditions are under attack. I will strive to help my culture evolve and flourish.

3. I will break the cycle of personal and cultural decay by ceasing my substance abuse.

4. I recognize my past errors and I will remember them when choosing a more noble and fulfilling path.

5. Having chosen a more noble and fulfilling path, I will strive to keep my errors in the past and correct errors and misjudgments as soon as they occur.

6. My heritage and my traditions give me a spirituality. By denying my heritage and my traditions, I deny my own self and may become vulnerable to relapse. By embracing who I am, I can better succeed in recovery and in life.

The Landmarks of the Path

1. We recognize who we are.

2. We acknowledge that our heritage, culture, and traditions are our strength.

3. We reject the vulnerability that comes from ignoring our roots.

4. We realize that others may have their own tradition and we respect them.

5. We understand that strength comes from embracing ourselves, not retreating from challenges.

6. Handsome Lake's example and advice may be useful to all who face personal disruptions.

Notes

NOTES

NOTES

0 1341 1571707 3

CPSIA information can be obtained at www.ICGtesting.com
Printed in the USA
LVOW02s2224270614

392146LV00001B/4/P

9 781593 118334